# Imperfect in an Uncertain World
## On Nonviolence

By Vanessa F. Hurst, MS

Wildefyr Press
Louisville, KY

Wildefyr Press
Louisville, KY 40242

Published in 2018.
Printed in the USA.

ISBN-13: 978-0-9908091-4-2

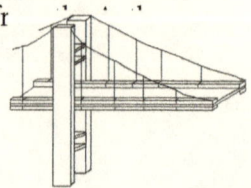

Thanks, Merlin for sharing your inner artist in your illustrations and layout; Barbara for your deep spiritual grace and proofreading, and to every person — family, friend, colleague, and intimate stranger that encourages me to live a nonviolent, compassionate life that is truly my message.

# Table of Contents

# Introduction

Imperfect. Uncertain. A Gate. Original Unity. My Message. My Life. What do these have in common? Each is an important component of living a nonviolent life. Each of us is imperfect. The world is uncertain. When we live without the barriers of divisiveness, our life, collectively and individually, becomes a message of hope, compassion, and nonviolent engagement.

When I developed and facilitated the course Merton On Nonviolence, I did not realize the impact the material would have on my students or myself. The insightful, engaging responses from the students led me to to capture the essence of the course in this workbook.

This workbook is a mosaic of nonviolence and compassion wisdom created with tiles from Thomas Merton, Dorothee Soelle, Mahatma Gandhi, Marshall Rosenberg, Pema Chödrön, and others, as well as my own experience. It begins with the premise that we are all imperfect beings navigating an uncertain world. We make this journey through the commotion and uncertainty by being attentive to the moment.

Imperfect in an Uncertain World: On Nonviolence is a journey through the uncertainty of the world and the acceptance of our imperfections to a place of peace and compassion. It provides tools that help you identify what triggers your violent reactions. It suggests activities that encourage development of a nonviolent, compassionate skill set. But, mostly, it shares a message of hope. We may be imperfect and the world uncertain, but we need not get stuck in the despair of either. We have the power to become whole and share our wholeness in the world. Within each of us is the power of transformation — to knit together our jagged edges torn by violence. That transformation to a less violent, more compassionate individuals who are the roots of a nonviolent world.

The workbook has four parts that build upon one another:

• Imperfect in an Uncertain World: We are all imperfect and the world uncertain. These factors lead to violent reactions. Reframe and re-script your life into one that is more compassionate and nonviolent
• The Gate of Nonviolence: This is not a gateway to the afterlife; rather, in this place we are our best, authentic self. In the gate we respond nonviolently and compassionately. Objectively heal the woundedness caused by suffering while uncovering the authentic in yourself and others.
• The Original Unity: We are increasingly siloed in our communities, our nations, and the world. Schisms have formed between nations and are based upon political ideologies and religious beliefs. Through a nonviolence stance, become collaborators and consensus builders who believe in the transformative power of compassion and peace.
• My Life Is My Message: Each of us has a message we share with the world. This is a connection of our intent and action. Although we may be imperfect and the world uncertain, our message can be one of hope. Power your transition from a movement of nonviolence into a way of living nonviolently through your intent and action.

You might be asking, "Why is a bonsai tree on the cover?" The illustrator recommended the image. A bonsai tree is a representation of the Japanese philosophy of wabi-sabi — the acceptance of imperfection and impermanence. Wabi-sabi invites us to recognize our imperfections as challenges and lessons that we learn on the journey of authenticity. Without wabi-sabi, we would be imperfect drowning in an uncertain world.

While the philosophy of wabi-sabi is not mentioned in this workbook, it is inherent in the message. Each of us is asked to recognize and accept our imperfections not as a vehicle of shame, but as means to become increasingly more authentic in this uncertain world. May your life message shine authentically from the messiness of your imperfections.

Vanessa F. Hurst, MS
December 2018

# Chapter 1

# Imperfect in an Uncertain World

We are imperfect beings living in an uncertain world. Our imperfections are what stop us from being authentic. These may be illusions about our self. They may be judgments or deep seated fears. It is not a person that triggers our reaction; rather our illusions, judgments, and fears do. For example, we might have very different political beliefs than another person. We may feel attacked by that person during a conversation. Or, instead of feeling attacked, we might hear what the person is saying, not take it personally, and respond with compassion.

No matter how much we ignore our imperfections, they do not disappear. We do not want to ignore or banish them from our life. Imperfections are tools to help us become our best, authentic self. They are challenges to meet and lessons to learn. Shifting our perspective from imperfections as unwanted flaws to important life tools, we are no longer stuck in feelings of failure and having unattainable expectations for our self.

With this acceptance, our paradigm shifts from viewing imperfections as a bane of our existence to engaging them as vehicles of growth. This is the beginning of self acceptance. Instead of seeing imperfections as personal failures, we reframe these parts of our self. They become opportunities to identify old wounds. This paradigm shift is paramount to healing our woundedness and living nonviolently in an uncertain world.

Once we heal our woundedness, we are longer trapped by imperfections. The window of our soul is cleaned, and, through it our authentic self reflects. With awareness and practice, our personal violence-induced flares lessen. Any acts of violence are met with a self compassionate response. Compassion for others is an outcome of self-compassion. We heal the world by first healing our self.

When we listen to our so-called imperfections, they have much to tell us about our illusions, judgments, and fears. They shine on what lurks in the shadows of our being. We discover what is hidden behind the illusion — our true, best self. Moving past the shadow of our imperfections, we become our true, best self.

The challenge inherent in each imperfection is to move past the fallacy of who "they" say we are and the illusions of who we believe we are into the person we truly are. This takes both courage and curious daring to look at our self and really see who we are — the authentic and the shadow. By challenging our imperfections, we stope being caught in an endless cycle of believing our illusions and reacting from them. Our illusions lose their power.

It is difficult to accept that we are imperfect. Acceptance begins by consciously identifying a single imperfection. We focus on something that is an illusion, a judgment, or a fear. For example, I have a fear that others will not like me. This fear manifests in my desire to be all things. When I do not feel my commitment is appreciated, I react. By listening to this imperfection, I can prevent an explosion of reaction by modifying my behavior — I no longer take responsibility for that which is not mine. With this awareness, I shift from a reaction to a response.

Listening to our self is key to understanding why we react and respond. It is the cornerstone of a nonviolent stance.

Now, it is your turn!

---

**Practice:** Listening to an Imperfection

**Part One**

- Identify something that you believe is an imperfection
- Recall how this imperfection has negatively impacted your life
- What did you tell yourself about it?
- How does it make you feel?
- Identify the challenge in the imperfection (if you are unable to identify the challenge, it is enough that you named the imperfection)
- How does the imperfection cause suffering in yourself?
- Reframe the imperfection in a way that makes you whole.
- What did the imperfection teach you?

**Part Two**

- Name an imperfection in another or in the world.
- What feelings of uncertainty did it trigger in you?
- How did you react to it?
- What did you tell yourself about the other?
- How did you feel toward the other?
- Identify the challenge in the imperfection (if you are unable to identify the challenge, it is enough that you named the imperfection)
- Where is the suffering in yourself or another in the imperfection?
- Reframe the imperfection to something that makes you whole and better able to respond to the uncertainty in the world.

---

With a stance of nonviolence, we intentionally identify and weed out the seeds of violence in our soul. To adopt this stance we need to know our self and use this knowing to cultivate a compassionate heart and a peaceful soul. By recognizing our triggers, acknowledging our suffering, and developing strategies, we are able to move from reactions into responses. Through awareness and diligence we become nonviolent warriors.

As a warrior of nonviolence our moment-by-moment battle is to recognize and root out violence in our hearts. Instead, we plant the seeds of peace. Each nonviolent thought, each compassionate action, nourishes the flowering of peace. We stop struggling against our imperfections and the uncertainty in the world as we grow nonviolent strong. While the world may be no less uncertain, and we no less imperfect; our default response is lovingkindness.

Very few people are actually malicious. Their "badness" is a manifestation of imperfections that are fueled by the need to make sense of uncertainty and their frustration of the inability to do so. When we exhibit "badness," we may even be stuck in the feelings of another or affective empathy. Unless we are attentive, we become a receptacle for their "badness" and enter a downward empathy spiral. We feel the emotions of another and are trapped in their suffering. Mired, we react violently.

All is not lost. We do not have to stay stuck in affective empathy. With mindful awareness, we recognize how the feelings of another catch us. We gain the power to move through empathy into compassionate response. As an objective observer, we no longer focus on imperfections and acerbate uncertainty. We defuse the violence and, in doing so, alleviate suffering in our self and others. We co-create a world of nonviolence.

Our journey to peace and compassion does not end with our ability to mitigate our violent reactions. We don't suddenly become an ever shining beacon of nonviolence in the world. Our awareness of the commotion in our self and the world grows. We recognize the bombardment of little and big triggers that impel us into violent reaction.

Heart committed to nonviolence, we navigate through the commotion by living in awareness. We are alert to the potential of seemingly inconsequential acts or words to trigger a violent outburst in our self or another. We become ever vigilant to our internal monologue. Our internal voice is no longer ignored or seen as benign. We acknowledge how it nurtures our seeds of violence. We rescript our internal monologue to soothe our wounded soul.

At issue is not the potential trigger; rather, it is our reaction to the trigger. It is not the other who causes our reaction, but our imperfection that catches us in reaction. We choose for a reaction to explode externally or to be snuffed out internally. In *Nonviolent Communication*, Marshall Rosenberg concurs with this: "What others say and do is a stimulus not the cause of our feelings" (Rosenberg, p 49).

Mindfully aware, we understand that we cannot eradicate the commotion feeding the roots of our triggers. We are able to navigate though the commotion with acceptance that we are not a superhero. We cannot control the words and actions of another. We can transform our reaction to them into responses. This transformation occurs with an identification of our triggers, the creation of strategies to minimize reactions, and a compassionate response.

For example, one trigger may be the fear that our imperfections will be uncovered and judged by another. We may feel diminished by the truth of our fallibilities and want to defend them at any cost. But, ignoring or justifying our imperfections never works. They smolder in the darkness waiting for a flash fire of indignation to lay waste to our peace.

Until we befriend our imperfections, our smoldering ember will forever be at risk of becoming wildfires. Instead of thoughts, words, and actions being sustained by love, they are depleted by anger. Our silence is consumed. Clarity is lost. Commotion overwhelms us. We are stuck in past fears or future worries. We are anywhere but where we need to be — in the moment.

We live in the ebb and flow of successfully navigating the commotion and being overwhelmed by it. We may go for extended periods responding with lovingkindness only to be caught unaware in a tsunami of reaction. The more we are mindful, the greater our ability to navigate through the illusions that propagate violence within.

Nonviolence becomes our superpower. With it, we respond from a place of heightened awareness and clarity. With each nonviolent thought, word, and action, we courageously accept our imperfections. But, we do not stop there. They become recognizable guides and chief navigators for our nonviolent journey.

As Thomas Merton reminds us, "mistakes are part of our life. …it is by making mistakes that we gain experiences. …the repeated experience has a positive value" (Merton, 128). Cultivating a nonviolent heart requires a shift from identifying our imperfections as "bad" or shameful to accepting them as guides. No longer adversaries or embarrassments, our imperfections become teachers of life lessons and a means to meet our challenges. Through them we live optimally and with purpose.

Once our imperfections are befriended, they become opportunities to practice gratitude. We can stumble about in a world filled with barriers to living a peace-filled life, or we can be grateful to the lesson each imperfection provides. As Pema Chödrön reminds us, "'Be grateful to everyone' is about making peace with the aspects of ourselves that we have rejected" (Chödrön, p 44). Making peace radically changes our life. We commit to a journey on which we learn from our imperfections and celebrate our authentic self.

Each imperfection reframed is as an invitation to be humble and vulnerable. We are free when we no longer hide or deny those less perfect parts of our self. Vulnerable, we acknowledge our fear while having the courage to seek the imperfection's message and the curious daring to respond to it. It takes humility to admit our wrongs and not be diminished by them. Humble and vulnerable, we objectively see the message embedded in those so-called flaws. Both traits foster objectivity. We discern the message of the imperfection and seek to understand how it is necessary to living our life purpose instead of triggering internal violence.

Violence does not begin "out there." Each of us has the capacity for internal violence to explode externally. This is an indisputable fact. The seeds of violence lay dormant within each of us. We may not even be aware of the seeds until they sprout in our words and actions. By the time they sprout, the roots of violence are deeply entrenched in the ground of our being. To eradicate the roots, we must turn inward.

The roots of violence are sustained by our thoughts, judgments, assumptions, beliefs, and defenses. When we listen to our internal monologue, we hear remnants of violence. Our judgments and beliefs spark fear and angst. Our nonviolent spirit erodes through angst and fear. We get so tangled in what we think ought to be that our only foreseeable recourse is violent reaction. Through full body listening (listening with all five senses) we identify the fears that trigger the violence in our internal monologue and navigate through the violence into peace.

**Full body listening** is attending with all of our senses and noting how they are manifest in our four aspects: body/mind/spirit/heart. We listen with not only our senses but with the aspects of our being. When we listen in this way, we notice how our physical body is impacted not only by our senses but by our spirit, emotions, and mind. We recognize how our body reacts to another's words or action. We may feel our chest tightening in trepidation when harsh words are spoken. We stand straighter when responding to words of praise. Our thoughts and emotions manifest in our bodies in a variety of ways including a muscle tick and a tickle in our throat.

One way to befriend our body is to practice being an objective observer or being in neutral. In this stance, we are more likely to notice when we are being triggered. We then can minimize our reactions and formulate responses.

Being nonviolent requires more than just preventing violent impulses from exploding. It involves aligning our body/mind/spirit/heart and responding through this integration. In alignment, we recognize the benefits of this stance. We are relaxed and peaceful. We notice how our mental and emotional bodies encourage peace or create stress. The more we experience peace and calm, the more we crave it.

A regular practice of compassion and nonviolence engenders peace in all four aspects. We eventually crave that feeling of calm. We notice our reactions to the uncertainty in the world. We are aware of a misalignment of the four aspects. With this awareness we are able to minimize the impact of reactions and compassionately respond.

Once we understand the roots of our fears and how they are fed by our judgments, assumptions, and defenses, we gain the ability to shift from reactionary violence to compassionate response. This shift is not automatic or easy. Through deep reflection, we better understand what informs our internal violence and how the commotion in the world triggers the explosion of internal violence into the external world. Through introspection, we rescript our response and deepen our nonviolent stance.

As we reflect and introspect, we examine our self internally noting how we react and respond to the external world. Reflection is objectively noticing how we are impacted. As we reflect, we are nonattached, non-judgmental, and non-defensive. Introspection is objectively putting together the pieces gained from reflection and creating a plan of action. Introspection requires critical thinking. To understand how our reactions stem from our internal violence, we ask:

- What do we fear?
- What illusions do we cling to?
- What truth do we push away?
- How do we judge?
- How does defending our actions result in violence?
- How do we blame and shame our self and others?

Through reflection and introspection, we discover how we nurture our internal violence in both easily identified and hidden ways. By owning our contribution to external violence we gain the power to shift into a nonviolent, compassionate paradigm. This transformation is impossible without humility, vulnerability, courage, and objectivity or being in neutral.

Each trigger recognized increases the power of our nonviolent presence. For example, I learned to identify how the anxiety of a friend was triggering an unkind reaction in me. When I spoke to her on the phone, I would be aware of physical sensations like a tightening in my chest. I learned that unless I could relax, I had about 10 minutes of connection before I reacted. If I could not shift my physical reactions, I knew when to end the phone conversation. I gained this understanding through reflection, introspection, and integration.

Understanding our triggers is key to reframing and rescripting our reactions into response. Now, it is your turn!

**Practice:** Recognizing Your Triggers

RI$^2$ is a contemplative practice that connects our body, mind, spirit, and heart (emotions) in ways that encourage compassionate response.

**To engage in RI$^2$:**

First, reflect with your heart. Identify what you feel without judging what you identify. Reflection is objective fact-finding.

Second, introspect using your logical mind. Ask yourself if there is a pattern to your behavior. Without judgment or defense, attempt to understand the root of your reaction. Through introspection, rescript the pattern to respond to your world.

Third, integrate what you learned in ways that shift fear-filled reactions to compassionate responses. More often than not, our transformation is a result of understanding the beliefs and judgments behind what we were thinking and intentionally stop acting out of preconceptions about our self or others. We reframe the world not to ignore the violence but to understand how internal and external actions feed our reactions.

The RI$^2$ process, practiced regularly, transforms us. Our thoughts, words, and actions are more reflective of our authentic self. We are more compassionate.

Use the following questions to reflect, introspect, and integrate a nonviolent stance into your own life. In a reflective place, notice the clues voiced in your quiet mind. Then engage in introspection noting how your responses reflect your authentic spirit and how your reactions creating illusions. Finally, integrate what you have learned.

- Think of a situation or person that triggers you.
- Reflect: how did the situation impact you? (be as specific as possible)
- Introspect: use what you learned during reflection to discover patterns, judgments, and beliefs that lay at the base of the trigger. How could you turn a potential reaction into a response?
- Integrate the knowing the next time the trigger surfaces.
- Note what word and what did not. Repeat the process to refine your responses.

We live in an uncertain world filled with commotion. Unless we open our self to the commotion, we are unable to be a beacon of nonviolence. Commotion is more than the distractions that pull us from the moment. It is the basis of challenges that triggers reactions or strengthens our peace. With humility, we can act upon the tumult to foster peace.

Thomas Merton recognized that "the humble man receives praise the way a clean window takes the light of the sun. The truer and more intense the light is, the less you see of the glass" (Merton, 112). The fog of commotion lifted, we see clearly through the window of our reality and shift from reaction to response. This shift is possible when we are aware of the commotion but do not react to it.

In the moment, we recognize the potential to slip into violent reaction. It is difficult to accept that we are a creator and sustainer of violence and that we contribute to the uncertainty. The truth is that with each breath we choose nonviolence or violence. It takes vulnerability to acknowledge when we lapse into violence. It takes courage to pull our self from the quagmire of commotion. With humility, we discern what triggered us and shift our reaction to nonviolent response. We accept that we are an imperfect being in an uncertain world.

Initially identifying our violent thoughts, words, and actions may be disheartening. To move through our frustrations and feelings of hopelessness requires humility and vulnerability. With humility, we accept that our acts do not define us; our reactions highlight imperfections we have not yet learned from. Vulnerable, we admit that not only are we imperfect but also that our behavior contributes to violence in the world.

It can be scary to admit how we contribute to the problem. It is empowering to realize how we are part of the solution. Being nonviolent is being courageously compassion to our self and others while radically transforming our self. To be nonviolent requires we balance our imperfections and the uncertainty of the world with nonviolent, compassionate response.

Radical transformation stems from reflection and introspection. Through it we identify our arrogance and self-righteous behavior. Pema Chödrön reminds us, "We are all capable of becoming fundamentalists because we get addicted to other people's wrongness" (Chödrön, Practicing Peace). Instead of being addicted to another person's wrongness, we identify our own wrongness, arrogance, and self righteous behavior. We name how these manifest as fundamentalism and acknowledge how they erode our nonviolent spirit.

We are never given an understanding of an imperfection without the knowledge to grow through it. Accepting our "wrongness" takes courage, vulnerability, and humility. As we reframe and rescript our life, we become less addicted to wrongness — ours and that of others. Our violent outbursts lessen; nonviolence becomes the base of our interactions. No longer hiding from or fearing our imperfections, we gain the flexibility to respond compassionately to uncertainties.

While we cannot control uncertainty in the world, with mindfulness we can temper our reactions to it. We gain the space to formulate nonviolent responses. There is an additional benefit in shifting from reaction to response. Each time we shift, we increase our response flexibility or our ability to minimize the impact of reactions. We recognize what triggers reactions and take steps to guard against those triggers.

With increased response flexibility, we navigate the dynamic messiness of the world. The need to be right and for another to be wrong no longer defines our interactions. Instead of judging and defending, we consciously seek ways to radically transform our self. In doing so, we trigger transformation in the world.

As we grow into our true self, we fear the roots of our violence less and less. We recognize that any moment of internal or external violence provides opportunity to respond with love and compassion. We have the power to nonviolently respond. In doing so, we no longer feed fear in our self and the world.

Fear is a byproduct of suffering. The way to alleviate fear is to alleviate suffering. Unless we alleviate our own suffering and fear, we are not able to alleviate the suffering of others. Self compassion is the compassion warriors most effective weapon. Only with a practice of self-compassion are we primed to share compassion with others. Self-awareness that grows from a practice of compassion deescalates turmoil and fosters peace.

Self awareness is a result of being an objective observer or being in neutral. When in neutral, we see the world without allowing our judgments to cloud our perception. When I know I am entering a highly charged situation, I spend a few moments centering myself and setting my intent to be objective. As a result I am more likely to catch my triggers before they create reactions. I rescript potential reactions into compassionate responses.

Remember, neutral is cultivated through practice. Now, it is your turn!

**Practice:** Being In Neutral

Use the following meditation to experience being in neutral.

Close your eyes...take a couple of breaths...become aware of your body...make a mental note of how your body feels....use your senses to describe the condition of your body...what does it feel like...how does it look...what sounds does it make...what does it smell like...how does it taste...where do you hold your tension...consciously relax...

Think of something that is very upsetting...find the place in your body where you are holding it...don't attach to the feeling...just be with it...no judgment...no defending...let the energy of the emotion dissipates...

Return to your breath...think of something very happy...go to that place in your body where you hold your happy thoughts... just be with it... allow the energy to dissipate...

Think of a neutral thought...something that you have no feelings about one way or another (Mine is the Detroit football team. I am so neutral on this one that I have no idea the name of the team.)...once you have that neutral thought, become aware of your body...where are you holding your neutral?...How does your body feel? Remember the feeling.

- Practice holding neutral so that when you are feeling a high emotion, you are aware and take steps not to react from it.
- Ask yourself what your body telling you. Don't cling to the answer. Release your fears. Formulate a response.
- The more your practice neutral, the easier it is to recognize when you are revving into reaction. You can use this space to shift into a place of neutrality and formulate a response.

---

The potential for nonviolence increases through the use of other tools for reflection and introspection. The 4nons increase awareness of how our imperfections trigger violence. The 4nons are non-attachment, non-judgment, non-defensive behavior, and non-violence.

- Non-attached, we are openminded and honest about what hooks us or what we shove away. We understand that to be truly non-violent, we must willingly and objectively experience violence, without reacting to it, in those moments when it catches us. We

are humble and vulnerable but do not consciously place our self
in harm's way. We experience violence in order to understand
how and why it hooks us. Being non-attached is an ongoing acknowledgment of how we get caught. Practicing non-attachment
means shifting our thoughts, words, and actions in ways that
ensure we are not caught.

- Non-judgmental, we recognize the good in everyone. We do not
  judge another or hold our self as better or more advanced. The
  goal of our actions is to understand suffering. We open to hearing
  the truth of another while understanding their perspective. To be
  non-judgmental, we must be non-attached.

- No longer defensive, we are humble, modest, and vulnerable to
  both our violent reactions and compassionate responses. We
  accept our imperfections without allowing them to define us. We
  recognize how an unawareness or denial of our imperfections
  informs our violent interactions and contributes to an uncertain
  world. When our energy is no longer spent defending our self,
  we no longer need to prove our self. We accept gratitude with
  an open heart. We recognize the sacred in each person and each
  event.

- The first 3nons are prerequisites to the fourth — nonviolence.
  Objective, without judgment, and non-defensive, we are gentle,
  forgiving, compassionate, and kind. We understand that love and
  compassion are what binds us together. If we destroy another
  with violence, we ultimately destroy our self.

Through the 4nons, we gain a greater understanding of the com-
plexity of our world. We recognize the components of our socially constructed reality (SCR). Our SCR is how we uniquely see the world. It is
based on our beliefs, judgments, and assumptions. It is influenced by our
family, culture, and tribe. We use this information to modify our SCR so
that it reflects our authentic core.

How we react and respond to the world is informed by our SCR.
Any illusions embedded in our SCR fuel our propensity to react with
violence. Refusing to get caught by those illusions, we are better able to
respond with compassion. With awareness, we see how our reactions
deepen our illusions and how our responses create a more authentic way
of seeing the world. We use this information to modify our SCR so that it
reflects our authentic spirit.

Now it is your turn! Learn how the 4nons or lack of them inform your SCR.

---

**Practice:** The 4nons

Practicing the 4nons is not easy. It requires courage and curious daring as we vulnerably accept our imperfections while issuing an invitation to others to co-create a peace-filled world.

Watch the news or read a news story while using the 4nons. Notice how you are

- getting hooked
- judging
- defending
- acting with violence

Then:

- Name what is hooking you.
- Reframe what you are seeing in ways that are non-attached, non-violent, non-defensive, and non-violent.
- How is your SCR changed to better reflect your authentic spirit?

---

By understanding how we form and sustain our SCR, we gain insight into the reasons we react and respond to another. We recognize that we react differently based on the judgments and assumptions that we make about people or situations. A friend may say the same thing as someone we do not like. We may engage the friend compassionately while attacking the other.

As we challenge the illusions in our SCR, we gain the ability to reshape our reality into a more accurate worldview. A reduction of illusions creates an SCR more in line with our true, best self. This reduction also prepares us to live imperfectly in an uncertain world.

Being nonviolent requires a deep awareness of who we are at our core. We no longer shy away from our imperfections. We learn from them. We modify our behavior in ways that reduce violent tendencies and increase our compassionate engagement. Looking at the world with authentic eyes, we minimize our reactions. Our interactions become more compassionate and nonviolent. The greatest challenge we may ever undertake is to be constantly vigilant against the causes of our violent outbursts. This vigilant awareness is the tipping point of our transformation.

Another tool that assists us in identifying what is true and what is illusory in our SCR is the Ladder of Inference. Developed by Harvard School of Business professor, Chris Argyris, the Ladder is a resource to better understand how individuals hear the same facts but come to different conclusions. Or, as Merton says, "you've got to look at the factors behind the facts" as we look at the beliefs, judgments, and assumptions at the base of an SCR (Merton, 123).

We use the Ladder to question our judgments and beliefs. The Ladder exposes our imperfections. Understanding how we move up and down the ladder, we identify the roots of our responses and reactions. The Ladder is more than a resource for understanding how we created and sustain our SCR. Using the information gained, we are able to reshape our SCR so that it better aligns with our authentic self. We respond compassionately to the world's uncertainty.

How we climb the Ladder of Inference:
- Each of us sees the same event as it unfolds
- We use personal filters to select data that strengthens our SCR
- We make assumptions based on our interpretation and how it validates of our worldview
- We draw conclusions that validate our SCR
- We form beliefs based consciously and unconsciously on how we see the world
- We act in ways that strengthen our SCR

We use the Ladder of Inference to challenge our beliefs, judgments, and assumptions. Using the Ladder in conjunction with RI2 and the 4nons helps us sustain an SCR best aligns with our true self.

The Ladder is a powerful tool for reflection and introspection. We use it unconsciously to interact with the world. Using it, we question if discarded information is truly unimportant. We see how ignoring certain information leads to a validation of our judgments, defenses, and assumptions. We note any triggers and subsequent reactions. It challenges us to recognize what is untrue and inauthentic. In doing so, we live in a reality that reflects who we truly are.

Now it is your turn! Let's see what you find on the rungs of your ladder!

---

**Practice:** Up and Down the Ladder

Reflect upon a time when your beliefs, judgments, and assumptions clashed with another. Think of a political, spiritual, or cultural difference.

Use the Ladder to identify the roots of your beliefs.

- What judgments, assumptions, and fears are at the root of your thoughts and actions?
- How they accurate?
- What is inaccurate?
- What is an illusion?
- Name the inherent violence.
- How has a change in your beliefs changed your SCR?
- How does this shift change how your interact with others?

---

The world is uncertain. We are imperfect. In order to live within the resulting commotion, our stance of nonviolence must be evolving and flexible. Just when we believe we have identified our imperfections, we are offered another opportunity to react. In this never-ending cycle, we recognize our imperfections and purge the roots of violence from our self. We continually question our motives and name our fears while being humble and vulnerable about the information gained.

We courageously choose what is most authentic. Becoming our best self takes more than the tools of the reflection and introspection, the 4nons, and the Ladder of Inference. It takes humility, vulnerability, courage, and curious daring. Through these core values and skills, we become an increasingly more nonviolent, compassionate, imperfect, authentic self who recognizes the gate of nonviolence everywhere.

# Chapter 2

# The Gate of Nonviolence

We live in two worlds — the uncertain, where our fears and angst are driving forces, and the extraordinary, where we power our actions with compassion. Within the uncertain, acts of violence percolate; within the extraordinary nonviolent revolution is birthed. We bridge these worlds by responding with compassion to imperfections and uncertainties. There is nothing magical about this bridge. It is crossed by our intent to be compassionate.

Uncertainty is exacerbated by inattentiveness. We fear what we do not know. When we are mindful, we better name our fears and see the extraordinary, a place where nonviolence is possible, shining in each moment. With an awareness of how we can be extraordinary, we shift from reaction to response. Through our lived experience of the extraordinary, we become change agents who use the power of our transformation to integrate the extraordinary into the uncertain.

In these moments of integration, we attune to the incredibleness of life unfolding. Although we live within the uncertainty, we see possibility shining from everything. Creating a nonviolent, compassionate world is no longer a maybe — we step along the pathway of nonviolence and compassion with our actions, words, and thoughts. The gate of nonviolence — a place of engaged compassion and peace — is revealed.

This gate is not just for a few who are able to experience it. It is available to all. The gate isn't a doorway to the great beyond. It manifests with peace and compassion in the here and now. In the present moment, we enter this gate through a shift in perspective. We accept that while we may always be imperfect and the world uncertain, we can choose to respond compassionately and nonviolently. This perception shift requires focusing our attention beyond the commotion to what really matters.

What really matters is our connection to one another and the vein of the sacred that flows through this connection. (For the purpose of this workbook, let's define the sacred as what we hold in great reverence.) Even if we cannot see the sacred in a person or situation, our response is an acknowledgment of what is there but not seen. With this acknowledgement, the gate of nonviolence is visible.

We attend to the world as a mystic. (For the purpose of this workbook, a mystic is open to the wonder and awe of life. A mystic experiences the sacred in all.) Our actions stem from a particular attention to the world. This attentiveness is a mystic experience. Being a mystic is living extraordinarily in an uncertain world. This way of being not for a select few. A mystic chooses not to live depending upon logic alone. Instead, their life is the total of their experiences of body, mind, spirit, and emotions.

Each of us has a mystic heart although some are unawakened. As a mystic, we do not negate our cognitive experience; rather, we have a full body awareness of the extraordinary. We experience the sacred somatically, mentally, and emotionally. We process our experiences cognitively and respond with our heart. This cycle from heart to head to heart powers our nonviolent responses to an uncertain world.

As a mystic, we practice a[3] awareness — being awake, alert, and alive.

- Being awake is more than getting up after a night slumber. When we wake, we are cognizant, conscious of both the uncertain and extraordinary of the world. We do not ignore or negate either. We notice possibilities to live fully. We are truly engaged. We have a soul understanding of our interdependence with everything in the world. By being awake, we gain the energy to be vigilant.

- Being alert is a state of vigilance. We bridge our intent to our action deliberately. When we live in the gate of nonviolence, our intent is to be compassionate and nonviolent. Our actions reflect this intent. We are mindful of opportunities to share our compassionate heart. We are aware of our triggers and their potential to cause violent outbursts. We navigate through the minefields of reaction into compassionate response. When we are vigilant, we may still react, but we learn from our actions. We rescript our reactions through compassionate action. Through our vigilance, we meet our challenges and learn our lessons. We are alive with purpose.

- Being alive is a result of being awake and alert. When we are alive, our reactions lessen and our response flexibility increases. We find it easier to recognize opportunities to respond with compassion and act nonviolently. We wake to the world. Mindfully noticing the suffering and the violence, we are compelled to transform our self and the world through nonviolence and compassionate presence. Alive, we enter the gate of nonviolence wherever we find it.

Awake, alert and alive, our attention is focused on the present moment. Alert and vigilant to the manifestation of the extraordinary in an uncertain world, we have the power to choose nonviolence and compassion. a³ awareness forges a path to our best, truest, most authentic self. We step readily into the gate of nonviolence and experience life as a mystic. Our choice is clear — to practice nonviolence and be compassion's presence in an uncertain world.

Being in a³ awareness takes practice. We get busy. Life intervenes. We find our self sleepwalking through the day. We notice opportunities to enter the gate. For example: I am often in a hurry at the store. One day in an effort to stop my frozen food from thawing, I offered to help a woman in front of me. We had a conversation about some of her health issues. Now, I am aware of the needs we all have to be seen and heard. I am also aware of of unseen suffering. Grocery shopping has become a community building experience for me.

Now it is your turn! Let's see how a³ awareness and the 4nons can change your socially constructed reality (SCR).

**Practice:** a$^3$ Awareness, the 4nons & Deepening Your Understanding of Your SCR

Choose a personal belief. Enter into a$^3$ awareness and use the 4nons (review pages 13-14). Be objective as you answer the following questions:

- In what ways are you attached to the belief?
- What judgments stem from this belief?
- What are your judgments about those who do not hold the same belief?
- How do you defend your belief?
- How are your actions, words, and thoughts violent toward those who disagree?

Choose a belief that you do not hold. Enter into a$^3$ awareness and use the 4nons.

- How are you averse to the belief?
- What are your judgments about those who do hold this belief?
- How do you defend your disagreement with the belief?
- How are your actions, words, and thoughts violent toward those who believe differently?

Now, using the 4nons while in a$^3$ awareness, come to better understanding about the differences in your beliefs and those of another. How can you share compassion to alleviate suffering in yourself and the other?

---

The paradigm shift to living nonviolently requires a heart-to-heart, soul-to-soul connection with our authentic self, others, the sacred, and all of creation. These relationships exist within an atmosphere of silence. This is more than a cessation of physical noise. In this environment of silence, we gain the clarity to understand how our imperfections and the uncertainty in the world births violence. For Merton, it was "necessary that we find the silence of God not only in ourself but also in another" (Merton, 86). When we connect with the sacred in each person and in each situation, we have the opportunity to mitigate violence with compassion and peace.

Silence is cultivated first in our self during moments of solitude. We become familiar with our internal chatter and sift through our thoughts to gain clarity. We separate our illusions and our distractions from what is true. Through mindfulness practice, we become adept in creating an environment of solitude wherever we are — be that alone or with others. Our silence becomes a shield we carry. It filters the illusions from what is real.

Through clarity gained, we transcend personal barriers that limit our compassionate presence. Barriers breached, it becomes easier to connect with others and enter the collect consciousness. This is a place of greater understanding gained through communal wisdom. In the collective, we better understand the truths of the others and the group. We are aware of any hidden agendas and motives. We encourage others to enter personal and collective silence in order to gain clarity. Through communally experienced solitude, we embody the authentic truth of the collective. Through this embodiment, we maintain an open gate of nonviolence. In the gate, we act in nonviolent and compassionate ways.

Within each of us is a spark of nonviolence, but obstacles prevent us from responding with this spark. We have emotional and mental wounds caused by deeply ingrained beliefs based upon illusions. Because of our wounds and the lack of rigid structure or guides to help us reach a place of peace and compassion, we may despair of ever being truly nonviolent. This despair is rooted in our blindness to our imperfections.

There is a way to live nonviolently. Through the cultivation of our solitude, we gain clarity. Our authentic self is our guide in developing a nonviolence stance. It empowers us to be vulnerable, humble, and courageous. With humility we name how our imperfections prevent the formation of a bridge from our intent to be nonviolent to compassionate action. Vulnerable, we no longer hide our inability to be a perfect bridge of nonviolence and compassion. We courageously accept our imperfections as we navigate nonviolently in an uncertain world.

With humility, vulnerability, and courage we follow the guidelines of Gandhi: "we do not wish ill, we refuse to cooperate with unjust groups, we are willing to sacrifice everything but our honor in order to create a life where nonviolence pervades everything" (Merton, Loc 1118). We acknowledge when we do not follow the guidelines and are compassionate to our self.

Following these guidelines we brings us to the threshold of the gate of nonviolence. We recognize that once in the gate we are unable to react violently. With awareness, our spark of compassion guides us. No longer do we view our imperfections as failures. Rather, they are opportunities to grow into our best possible self.

Growing into a less violent self, we engage in lifelong learning by reframing our reactions to compassionate responses. Instead of being addicted to another's wrongness or our wrongness, we become addicted to the nonviolent potential in all. This potential resonates from our body, mind, spirit, and heart lighting our path. We enter the mystic's path, a place of hyperawareness and attentiveness to the world. As a mystic, participating in violence becomes distasteful and even emotionally, mentally, and physically painful.

Embracing our mystic heart, we live in the gate of nonviolence. We are compelled by our authentic spirit to respond with compassion. We become de-escalators of violence. We choose nonviolent action by listening with the ears of our heart, seeing with the eyes of our soul, and speaking with the tongue of our\ spirit. This is the mystic's default form of communication. Although a mystic may physically live in uncertainty, we respond through our connection to the extraordinary. In our response to the world, others experience the gate of nonviolence.

Through our connection to others and all of creation, we deepen our mystic relationship with the extraordinary. Our journey as mystic begins through a connection to the sacred and strengthens through interactions with others. We connect to the extraordinary divine spark to divine spark. (The Legend of the Divine Spark: When each soul was conceived, the Creator carved off a piece of Itself and blew this spark into the soul. This act awakens each of us to the mystic journey through the uncertainty into the extraordinary. This carved off piece is our divine spark.) As a mystic, we seek to awaken the divine spark in others and, in doing so, spread peace and compassion throughout the world.

Maintaining a stance of nonviolence is possible through the cultivation of silence and becoming comfortable with our solitude. When I spend time each morning in contemplative practice, I am more aware of my potential to cause harm. This awareness empowers me to choose reaction or response.

Now it is your turn! The following helps you to somatically, emotionally, and mentally connect to your divine spark.

**Practice:** Cultivate Silence, Connect to the Divine Spark

Spend a few moments breathing...visualize your divine spark...
what does it feel like? ...what does it look like? ...what does it sound like?
Set your intent to follow your breath to your Divine Spark...Take
a couple of breaths...do not try to shift your breathing...just notice your
breath...allow the air to flow through your body...rest in the quiet...go
to the place where your divine spark resides...notice what prevents you
from fully connecting to your divine spark...name your attachment...
notice how you attach...what are your judgements about your ability to
rest in the silence...what defenses do you have about what is happening...
with each inhale, breathe peace and quiet into your being...exhale your
anxieties, your fears, the roots of your violence...be with your breath for
several minutes...

Once calm, engage your breath...allow it to flow to the site of
your Divine Spark...rest in the light of your spark...listen with your senses to what it is telling you...what do you see...what do you hear...what do
you smell...what do you taste...what do you feel? Note what you sense...
follow the connection between your spark and the extraordinary...be
filled with compassion and nonviolence.

How did it feel to rest in silence?
How did it feel to connect to your divine spark?

Practice this once a day for a week. How do your interactions
with other and yourself shift?

Within an environment of silence, we gain clarity in order to
experience life authentically. Our internal spark flares with a nonviolent
response. Merton described this spark as a "point of nothingness." He
reminds us that, "At the center of our being is a point of nothingness
which is untouched by sin and by illusion, a point of pure truth, a point
or spark which belongs entirely to God... This little point of nothingness
and of absolute poverty is the pure glory of God in us... It is like a pure
diamond, blazing with the invisible light of heaven" (Merton, 148). This
divine spark is the originator of our nonviolent stance.

Merton affirms, "It is in everybody, and if we could see it, we would see these billions of points of light coming together in the face and blaze of a sun that would make all the darkness and cruelty of life vanish completely. ...I have no program for seeing. It is only given. But the gate of heaven is everywhere" (Merton, 148). Imagine what our life would be like if we could be part of a collective ablaze with these points of light. We would discover a world of gates. These are places of nonviolence.

We enter the gate of nonviolence through the guiding light of our divine spark. The gate is further illuminated when we join together with others. This community of divine sparks creates a compassionate world of peace by eradicating the seeds of violence. To live in a nonviolent community, we create peace first within our self and then nurture nonviolence in community.

Within our little point of nothingness is unconditional love — our driving force. Living from this spark, we experience freedom from hate, vengeance, and discord. Within our solitude we practice unconditional love and strengthen our awareness of the divine spark until we no longer need seek the gate of nonviolence. We recognize that we are living in it. Mystic eyes open, we have the power to transform an uncertain world into an extraordinary place of nonviolence and compassion.

As a mystic we walk between the uncertain world and the extraordinary. We recognize how the uncertainty and the resulting violence depletes us. Experiencing life as a mystic increases our awareness of the detrimental effects of violence on our spirit. We feel what violence does to our body, mind, spirit, and heart. Free of a constant barrage of violence, a mystic seeks to live in the energizing place of nonviolence. With mystic eyes we see clearly and live in ways that give us strength to withstand the bombardment of uncertainty and violence.

As a mystic, we seek the sacred in every interaction — uncertain or extraordinary. We connect to the divine spark of not only people but of the action itself. We understand that everything has a part of the sacred in it. In this recognition we gain the ability to alleviate suffering and reduce the residue of nonviolence.

We live from our authentic core realizing that the actions of another say more about them than they say about us. We no longer take the actions of another personally. We understand that each harmful action is a result of fears and judgments. They are reflections of an SCR created and sustained by the journey up and down the Ladder of Inference. This inner knowing reduces our angst. Using this wisdom we navigate through potential reactions to a loving, gentle response. This response radically transforms us and provides the impetus for world transformation.

As a font of nonviolence and compassion, our mystic heart is humble and vulnerable. Our response to conflict in relationship shifts. Instead of being caught in arrogance or judgment, we understand reactions stem from the internal roots of external actions. We courageously commit to identifying and understanding the suffering of another. We realize that any violence encountered, somatically, mentally, emotionally, or spiritually, is an opportunity to practice nonviolence. And, an opportunity to empower another to be peace.

Identifying the roots of violence is not as important as recognizing that violence is a reflection of the woundedness of individuals and the collective. The mystic choice of nonviolence is the only way to heal the world's wounds. We are attentive to suffering without needing to know the cause. Understanding the roots of violence is a bonus. Each alleviation of suffering provides resources to heal the roots of suffering — whether known or unknown.

In the gate of nonviolence, we discover a "new relation to the three powers that imprison us: ego, possession, and violence" (Soelle, loc 3516). Free, we live in this new mystic paradigm of humble discovery. We are hyperaware of our compulsion to cling or push away — we realize that either action creates a possession and the potential for violence within the possession. Not getting caught in possessions requires attention in the moment.

Our mystic commitment is to deepen our humility while being courageous and vulnerable. We become increasingly aware of how ego, possessions, and violence draw us away from the moment and weaken our connection to the divine spark. We recognize the illusions that draw us farther away from the gate of nonviolence. To reconnect, we humbly acknowledge our imperfections, practice self compassion, and courageously navigate uncertainty.

Blinders removed, we see with eyes of the heart and hear with the ears of the soul. As a mystic, we understand that our fears and imperfections do not define us. They present challenges to be courageously met. Once met, our imperfections become our strength. We understand that "our deepest fear is that we are powerful beyond measure. It is our light, not our darkness that most frightens us…" (Williamson, 190).

We do not walk the path of uncertainty alone. The way through fear is lit by our divine spark and the sparks of others. As a mystic in the gate of nonviolence we recognize that we cannot succeed alone. The energy of the sparks of others empower our nonviolent spirit. When we are aware of the divine that rests within everyone, we no longer need to prove our self. Our fear diminishes when we recognize that we are in the gate of nonviolence each time we practice compassion.

Perhaps the greatest challenge to being nonviolent is our attachment to things, people, dogma, and beliefs. They are the underpinnings of our fundamentalism. When I have conversations, I listen to what in the other's comments catch me. When I find missteps on my Ladder of Inference, my SCR shifts.

Now it is your turn! What catches you?

---

**Practice:** What possessions keeps you stuck

Possessions are more than the material objects. Possessions may be emotions we cannot let go, an internal monologue that plays on an unending loop, or a connection to another that is no longer life sustaining.

Name one possession that you have — it may be physical, emotional, mental, or spiritual.

- How is it feeding the seeds of nonviolence?
- What illusion grows from it?
- What are your fears about letting it go?
- What little ways can you stop being attached to it?

---

As a mystic we become a nonviolent resister who speaks out against injustice not with violence but with lovingkindness. We do not wish ill or engage in unjust activities. We are willing to sacrifice everything but our authenticity in our intent to be nonviolent. Nonviolence pervades every thought, every word, and every action. We hear the voice of our divine spark nudging us to let go of any violent tendencies. We feel the damage of violence somatically, mentally, emotionally and spiritually. We are still imperfect, but we seek to become imperfectly nonviolent.

As we heal the wounds of violence, our paradigm shifts. We intentionally create a life based on causing no harm and alleviating suffering. We are deliberate in choosing every thought, word, and action. We understand nonviolence begins with us. While practice may never make us perfect, we recognize that through practice we gain the awareness to live imperfectly in an uncertain world.

To be a mystic is to enter into a compassionate relationship with the world. Our relationship with the Sacred becomes less about a one-to-one connection with the divine. All becomes sacred to us; we are connected to the sacred through all. We no longer take the actions of another personally. We understand that each of us provides challenges for others.

We feel our body/mind/spirit/heart connection to all and acknowledge the interdependence of life. The sacred is reflected in every part of our life. We acknowledge the sacred as a third partner in all relationships. With this understanding any relationship we engage in occurs in the gate of nonviolence.

We are empathetic in all our interactions because, for a mystic, empathy is a radical transformer. A mystic experiences the world with their full empathic being — body, mind, spirit, and heart. Chuang Tzu said that "empathy is listening with the whole being" (Rosenberg, loc 1834). As a mystic, we experience empathy — listening and acknowledging the sufferings and joys around us — with all four aspects of self. We are aware of the feelings of others and respond compassionately to their feelings.

We hear with our full body even when we are not aware of the conversation. Unfortunately, unless we are aware, we may be unable to articulate what our body is hearing. Deaf to our reactions, we are stuck in affective empathy and are unable to move into cognitive empathy. Nonviolence or compassionate action seems out of our reach.

Living in a$^3$ awareness, we are less likely to get stuck in affective empathy. Awake, alert, and alive, we notice how the suffering or even violence of another is impacting us somatically, mentally, emotionally, and spiritually. We have the power to stop the impact of violence by using tools that increase our objectivity and mindfulness.

**Affective empathy** is our emotional response to the feelings of another. When we are unaware, we get stuck in feelings of sympathy. We may believe the feeling of another are ours. Stuck in empathy, our feelings have the potential to fatigue us. We are unable to recognize the origin of what we are feeling. In an effort to break free of the fatigue, we may react violently.

When we are aware that we are experiencing the emotions of another, we move from affective empathy to **cognitive empathy**. Acknowledging that empathetic feelings are not ours but echoes of another's and recognizing the origin of these feelings is cognitive empathy. Once in cognitive empathy, we are able to objectively formulate a compassionate response. Bridging affective empathy to cognitive empathy releases the potential of reactionary behavior and creates the space for compassionate, nonviolent response to thrive.

Using the 4nons, non-attached, non-judgmental, non-defensive, and non-violent, we enter into neutral and lessen the impact of another's emotions on us. We do not get stuck in the feelings or cast them away with aversion. We do not judge the other for how they experience their predicament. If we find our self caught in the emotions of another or are unable to empathize, we do not defend our self. Through empathy we foster a gentle, forgiving, kind, and compassionate way of responding. Our empathy is a shining light within the gate of nonviolence that invites others to be nonviolent.

We are imperfect. This world is uncertain. No matter how mindful we are, it is inevitable that we get stuck in affective empathy. We react not from our true self but from violence fueled by illusion. When we are unaware and caught in regrets, worries, hopes, or fears, we lose sight of the present moment. We are no longer objective. The gate of nonviolence seems closed to us. But, do not despair. The gate is always there waiting for a mystic's open eyes and an objective knock.

Being objective roots us in our authentic being. One way to maintain our objectivity and our connection to the gate of heaven is through 90-seconds of clarity. Jill Bolte Taylor in My Stroke of Insight discovered that the life span of an emotion is 90-seconds. This is the average time that it takes an emotion to move through the nervous system and out of the physical body. Unfortunately, instead of moving through the cycle of an emotion, we may hold on to an emotion. It spirals into our body, mind, spirit, and heart causing fatigue. What should last 90-seconds lasts 9 minutes, 9 month, or even 9 years.

We can use this 90-seconds to our benefit by engaging in full body listening for 90-seconds. During that time we notice how the emotion impacts us. We do not attach, judge, or defend the emotion. We are with the emotion objectively and nonviolently. Often, after 90-seconds, the emotion's impact on our body is greatly minimized.

Through the power of 90-seconds, we gain information about how the emotions of another impact us. This understanding boosts our power to respond nonviolently. By moving into neutral, an objective place of noticing, we are better able to  recognize the bombardment of commotion and create strategies to lessen the impact of violence.

As a mystic we understand the many ways the sacred permeates our lived experience. "See I give you my eyes that you may feel all things with them, and my ears, that you may hear all things with them, my mouth I also give you, so that all I have to say, whether in speech, prayer, or song, you may say through it. I give you my heart, that through it you may think everything and may love me and all things for my sake" (Soelle, Loc 3987). Mechthild von Hackeborn clearly outlines how a mystic experiences the sacred. When we develop our solitude, we connect to our mystic heart. In this place of clarity, we experience reverence in each moment. Our ability to react from our fears and anger is lessened.

With our continuous experience of the sacred, we unravel the roots of violence. Our socially constructed reality shifts through our intentional looks at life. We reflect upon the ways that we judge and assume. We consciously make efforts to stop judging and defending, blaming and shaming. We experience every moment while in relationship the sacred. We live Gandhi's words, "love is the law of our being" (Merton, 341). We love all unconditionally for we recognize that this way is the only true path in an uncertain world.

Have you ever held on to a hurt, an anger, or a fear for longer than 90-seconds? Did you get to a point where you didn't know how to live without it? I know that I have. Not only did it draw my attention from the present moment, but the suffering that resulted from clinging to the emotion was exhausting. I have found moving into neutral helps me stay in the commotion while not getting attached to it. Resting in my solitude, I identify what is catching me and what has the potential to catch me. With this awareness I circumvent being stuck in uncertainty and my imperfections.

Now it is your turn! How can you let go of the barbs of commotion?

---

**Practice 90-Second:** Letting Go the Bombardment of Commotion

(You may need to practice the Neutral Exercise, on page 13, in the first chapter before trying this one.)

Close your eyes...take a couple of breaths...become aware of your body...recollect a time when you were caught in the emotions of another...notice how the memory of those emotions are still impacting you...notice how you are caught it them...this may manifest in a particular part of your body...you may have anxious thoughts...notice how you attempt to push them away...name how you are judging the other...identify how you are defending your thoughts...

Connect with your divine spark...rest in the center of calm...breathe in peace...

Find your place of neutral...hold that space as you move from affective empathy to cognitive empathy...name how you can alleviate your suffering...how you can alleviate the suffering of another...feel your body/mind/spirit/heart calming...allow the well of compassion to move through you...be self compassion...practice compassion to others...

- How did the emotion catch you?
- Did you notice any fatigue?
- If so, where was it?
- How were you able to move from affective to cognitive empathy?
- It this helpful? Why or why not?

---

Loving another does not mean that we do not hold them accountable for their action. Loving is perhaps the most difficult act. We see the violence in the world, love the perpetrator, seek justice, and act to eradicate violence. The mystic path of resistance requires a creative, change agent mentality that responds to the uncertainty in a dynamic, evolving manner. There is no template for this. A mystic follows the inner wisdom shining from their heart.

When love is the law of our being, every act of violence, every burst of anger becomes a wake up call. They are reminders that we are not living with a3 awareness. We are stuck in the uncertainty of the world. But, we need need not stay stuck. Marshall Rosenberg suggests that when we identify anger, a precursor to violence, that we stop and breath. Next, we identify judgmental thoughts and honestly connect with our needs. Finally, we nonviolently express our feeling and unmet needs (Rosenberg, loc 2725). Through these simple steps we deescalate anger before it erupts into reaction and the resulting violence cascades into the world.

---

**Practice:** Stop and Breathe

Call to mind a time when you were angry and unable to control your reaction to it. Hold the memory. Then

- Stop and breath
- Identify judgmental thoughts
- Connect with any need that is not met in that moment
- Nonviolently express your feeling and unmet needs (even if you just express these to yourself.)

* from *Nonviolent Communication* by Marshall Rosenberg

- Did this practice help you release the triggers of reaction?
- If so, how?
- What remains of the memory?

---

A mystic resister is not cloistered from the world. As a mystic we experience the sacred not only personally but within the interdependence of life. We walk within the uncertainty while residing in the gate of nonviolence. Our journey is powered by our nonviolent heart and compassionate soul. We share peace and compassion with all in the world. By embracing the path of the mystic, we humbly serve as a model for a world filled with imperfections and uncertainty.

# Chapter 3

# The Original Unity

No matter how determined we are, how much we change, we cannot transform the world by our self. Our transformation is but one stone in the foundation of a nonviolent society. Modifying the African proverb "it takes a village to raise children" to "it takes a village to live nonviolently" is the cornerstone of a nonviolent, compassionate world.

It takes a collective of determined, radical transformers to shift a societal paradigm. While we may only be able to change our self, sharing our lived experience with others has the potential to bring about change in others. Authentic, compassionate relationships are necessary to create peace. Through these relationships we return to the original unity. We accept that we are and have always been one.

Even when we collectively work toward a common goal, the world is still uncertain and each of us imperfect. Together in community we support one another despite our imperfections and through the uncertainties. Each of us shows up humble and vulnerable. We practice self-compassion and share compassion with others. With a collective of compassion we support each other on the path through life's uncertainty. The journey we take may be no less scary, but our courage is multiplied when we part of a compassion collective.

A community of nonviolence just doesn't happen. We don't join together and suddenly are collectively nonviolent in our thoughts, words, and actions. It is built through intentions of individuals and the conscious actions of the collective. It is sustained through individual and group compassionate action and mindfulness. When in community, the goal is to be our truest self. We are aware of our authentic self and the illusions that dilute our authenticity. We realize that unless we are honest about who we are, authentic and shadow, we are unable to fully connect with others in community. We realize that the potential for violence to erupt exists in each unaware moment.

Being in community requires that we show up authentically. In doing so, we strengthen the fragile bonds of connection through listening intentionally and responding compassionately. This nonviolent, compassionate communication is woven with respect, humility, and vulnerability. Through compassionate communication, we strengthen the collective consciousness and minimize the impact of reactions.

---

The **collective consciousness** holds the shared beliefs and the values of a group of people. It is the repository of what individuals have in common. It is the great unifier.

---

Once in the collective consciousness, we engage in communion. Although this form of communication may include verbal communication, it supersedes words. Communion is an outcome of listening intentionally and responding compassionately. Its practice opens us to really hearing what the other is saying. We understand how our beliefs, judgments, and agendas may be preventing us from fully engaging in community.

In communion, we hear the words within the context of body language, inflection, and emotions triggered in us. We recognize that less than 10% of what is heard in a conversation is the actual spoken words. The other 90% is what we perceive with our other senses. Communion asks us to engage another with our body, mind, spirit, and heart in order to hear what is said nonverbally.

Through communion we create an active, vibrant, collective consciousness. Community members focus on the common good. Although we still use words, our way of interacting expands to include nonverbal, compassionate communication. We hear words, notice body language, and recognize the meanings of body language. We intuitively understand what the other is saying. We seek clarification. We verify our understanding through nonviolent, compassionate responses and intentional queries. Communion requires that we become comfortable with pockets of silence that occur when we intentionally listen instead of rushing to respond.

A Community of nonviolence lives the original unity that Thomas Merton recognized, "My dear brothers and sisters, we are already one" (Burton, 308). This older unity is echoed in the myth of our conception:

at the conception of our spirit, the Creator carved off a bit of Itself and blew this piece, our divine spark, into each of us. Connecting divine spark to divine spark is key to communion and weaving the threads of nonviolence into community.

Connecting to others with communion requires intentionality, humility, and vulnerability. We willingly set aside our agendas and open to transformation even if it does not look the way we want. We are clear in our intent while being aware when our motives are not in alignment with it or the intent of the community. When we are aware that our intent is not in alignment, we are vigilant about not forcing our agendas upon the group.

It is easy to tell our self that we have no ulterior motives for our actions — even when our motives are positive and compassionate. Upon reflection, we may discover that our motives for our nonviolent actions have shadow components. We may wish for accolades or some kind of recognition for our good deeds. Or, we may act compassionately so others see that side of us. Although this motive does not prevent us from being nonviolent, it sows the seeds of violence in us. When we act in ways that are not humble or vulnerable, we create cracks in our spirit through which violence takes root.

---

### Intent vs. Motive

Our intent is our goal while our motive is the reason we do something. We may be nonviolent to create a peaceful world (a goal) or nonviolence may be a way to promote our personal agenda. (a motive)

---

Even with the best intentions, it may be difficult to separate our intent to be compassionate and nonviolent with our motives. For me, it is difficult to practice the compassion of enough. I might believe that I am doing everything in my power to alleviate suffering when in fact I enable the person to ignore the roots of their suffering. My intent to alleviate suffering gets tangled in my desire to fix the person who is suffering.

Now it is your turn! To eradicate the roots of violence, name the seeds from which they grow.

**Reflect** upon a time when your intent to be compassionate was diluted by your motives.

- What was your ulterior motive or agenda for being compassionate?
- Did you realize the motive/agenda prior to your action?
- If not, when did you become aware of your motive/agenda?
- How did you become aware?
- How did you feel after sharing what you thought was compassion?
- How did it differ from when you were compassionate without an ulterior motive?
- How can you prevent your ulterior motives from informing your actions?

As a member of a nonviolent community, we practice a³ awareness. We are awake and alert to our motives and agenda. We consciously strive to minimize any negative impact on the collective's work for the common good. As collaborators we are aware of how our personal motives, judgments, and personal desired outcomes might prevent us from attaining the common good. In our interactions with one another, we are humble and vulnerable. We listen with intent and respond with compassion as we work toward the goal of creating a better, less violent world.

Spend time asking how your personal socially constructed reality meshes with the reality of the group. While the SCRs have commonalities, they probably are not identical. Ask how your SCR and the collective SCR is compatible. Discern if you can authentically shift your reality closer to that of the collective. The SCRs of individuals and the group need not be the same, but they should have common points and the ability to interface.

As a member of community it is important that we balance our needs with the needs of the group. Our personal agendas should not impede the group's ability to work together. Our goal as a community member is to reach consensus. This does not mean that every group member is 100% in agreement or is in alignment with the group's vision, mission, and values. A nonviolent community is diverse and inclusive. It is a mosaic of SCRs of individuals who come together with a common goal — nonviolence and compassion. In time, we might find an organic evolution of individual SCRs as they more closely align to one another's and the group's.

A group of individuals committed to living through a collective consciousness is no longer willing to settle with compromise. Although it is easy to create strategies and plan when compromising, the pitfalls of this form of team building are easily identified. With compromise, theoretically, each side gives a little and everyone meets in the middle. When the goal is not reached or a solution is not viable, there is often resentment from individuals or group factions. With compromise there might be feelings of unevenness — that one party may believe that it gave too much while the other gave too little. With this comes the risk of blaming and shaming.

Instead of working toward compromise, a nonviolent community focuses on reaching consensus. Working toward consensus asks us to shift our approach of goal setting and resolution making. Instead of anticipating a compromise, we commit to discovering the most appropriate resolution for the group. This may mean that the end product looks nothing like what any faction wanted. In fact, it may be an idea that no one thought was viable until everyone brainstormed potential possibilities. Consensus is a fruitful, transformative way of engaging and strengthening the collective.

Working to create consensus requires showing up as your best, most authentic self while agreeing to work within the collective consciousness while being aware of our motives and agendas. Collaborating with consensus in mind means intentionally working together. No longer separate individuals desiring the best outcome according to their personal SCR, the group becomes a single entity striving toward the collective good.

With a focus on consensus, the collective travels a path of internal nonviolence. While the world may still be uncertain, consensus opens the gates of nonviolence. As a group we grow community in the gate. We remain there by communally committing to collective nonviolence. This means that we are gentle and loving as we hold our self and others accountable for harmful or hurtful behavior. As consensus builders, we are a community of compassion.

As we use skills such as consensus building, our ability to be nonviolent both as an individual and as a community member continues to evolve. No longer focusing on a narrow scope of possibilities, we open to all that is possible. We accept that we are not perfect. We recognize that we cannot expect anyone or community to be perfect. We accept Gandhi's words as our own, "We may never be strong enough to be entirely non-violent in thought, word, and deed. But, we must keep non-violence as our goal and make steady progress toward it" (Merton, Loc 562). Gandhi understood even in moments of imperfection and uncertainty, we intentionally take step by nonviolent step. We are less likely to take a detour when journeying with others who are committed to nonviolence.

Through each nonviolent act, we evolve into our most authentic self. As we collaborate with others, we empower community to evolve authentically. In this community of consensus, we lift others up instead of negating where they are on the journey. We are aware of how blaming and shaming, judging and defending, are roots of internal and external violence. With compassion we circumnavigate our judgmental reactions. Compassion is the foundation of growing a nonviolent life as we shift from reaction to response.

Violence sneaks up on us when we are unaware. We might only realize how our anger caught us after we utter words or acted. Instead of holding on to our imperfections, the time to act is immediately following an expression of violence. We identify the roots of our violence and identify the seeds. In this way we heal our wounds and grow into our nonviolent self and empower nonviolence within community.

Now it is your turn! Although this may be a painful exercise, please engage. After you complete it, remember to practice self compassion.

---

**Practice:** Reflect upon a time that you were stuck in anger that you directed toward a person or a group.

- What was at the root of your anger?
- How did you hold a grudge?
- What were your acts of revenge?
- How did your acts of revenge nurture the seeds of violence?
- Were you able to move from violence to nonviolence? If so, how?
- If you were unable to shift, what steps can you take to begin shifting to a nonviolent stance?
- If you believe that we are all one, how does your behavior shift?

We no longer enable bad behavior. Instead we alleviate suffering. We hold others and our self accountable for unacceptable behavior. We alleviate both the suffering that triggered the behavior and the suffering that resulted from the action. We share compassion with both parties for we recognize the truth in Gandhi's words: "there will never be an army of perfectly nonviolent people. It will be formed of those who will honestly endeavor to observe non-violence." (Merton, loc 40). We recognize that the gate of heaven is visible when we stand with others who endeavor to be nonviolent. We forgive the cause of suffering, accept the imperfections, and practice self compassion.

The way to successfully navigate uncertainty is to recognize that each of us, complete with our own imperfections, are in this together. When we, individually and collectively, are vigilant in our thoughts, words, and actions, we create an environment where love and compassion are the norm. This doesn't mean that all acts of violence stop. It means that we unconditionally accept the other while encouraging the release of violence in their hearts. We become an active member of a community of compassionate accountability.

Understanding that we are all one leaves no room for vengeance. Revenge is a product of the illusion that we are separate. If we are truly one, how can we seek revenge? We cannot unless we wish to perpetrate violence. Banishing this illusion of separateness, the path to compassion and nonviolence clears. As a community, we collectively work together in ways that all benefit. Our response as individuals, group members, and the community at large is evolved nonviolent compassion.

Shifting from vengeance to nonviolence requires an awareness of empathetic feelings. We notice when we are sensing the emotions of another. We discern how those feelings are impacting our feelings. We practice a3 awareness to discern how our feelings get tangled in another's suffering. This awareness is necessary for us to hold our calm center and not being swept away by our angst and fear.

We all experience empathy, but we may be unaware of what the feeling represents or that the feeling is not ours. If we are unaware, we get stuck in affective empathy or a state of feeling the emotions of another. Being stuck may trigger our frustrations, fears, and anger. We may be carried away by the feelings and lash out at others. Or, we may be filled with a suffering that is not ours and that we are unable to alleviate. Being part of a community can help us move from affective empathy to cognitive empathy. Through the collective consciousness we discover ways to name the origin of the emotional and work together to alleviate the resulting suffering.

We are not alone in experiencing empathy or our own suffering when we are in community. The collective consciousness helps us identify when and how we get stuck. The values and beliefs of the group can be instrumental in moving us from affective empathy or the feelings of another to cognitive empathy where we acknowledge those feelings. In cognitive empathy, we name the emotion without taking ownership. We actively identify the suffering of another and then act with compassion. In community, we do not act alone. We engage the community's collective compassionate heart to alleviate suffering.

When violence happens in a group, it is often a result of herd mentality. Riots are a product of herd mentality. People seemed to be carried away by the angst and anger of others. Is it possible to shift from a herd mentality of violence to a herd mentality of nonviolence and compassion? I believe it is. The paradigm shift requires conscious intent and an awareness of a group's emotional temperature. When I remain anchored and shielded, I am less likely to be carried away by collective emotions. When I recognize that I am being carried away, entering the quiet and being an objective observer brings me back into the moment.

Now it is your turn! Practice the following exercise alone and then in groups — one that is tense, another that is calm.

---

**Practice:** A Herd Mentality of Nonviolence

When you are in a situation where emotions are running high, begin to breathe deeply and evenly. Relax your physical body as much as possible. Notice your thoughts but do not engage them. Name where your emotions are stuck. When you are feeling more objective, visualize that you are a font of peace and compassion that overflows into the people present and the situation. Be aware of how you continue to be triggered. Practice the 4nons (nonattached, nonjudgmental, nondefensive, and nonviolent). Do not engage violence with violence. Notice what happens to those around you.

You can practice this with one person or more. In fact, practice this with a group that is having no seeable problems and notice what happens. Can you bring increased peace to a calm group?

---

As an emissary of nonviolence, we recognize the futility of forcing change in the so-called adversary. Instead, we take Thomas Merton's advice to "turn them from an adversary into a collaborator by winning them over" (Merton, 12). Badgering someone into change never works. A nonviolent community is a diverse, inclusive one. We accept all for who they are while encouraging them to address their shadow and be their best authentic self.

Mindfully welcoming the so-called adversary into discussion provides opportunities for the evolution of our self and the other into increasingly less violent people. With openness, members of community learn about the socially constructed views of reality of others. Their Ladders of Inference are challenged. In doing so, the community has the potential to become increasingly more flexible, more inclusive, and welcoming.

The adversary is no longer *other* for we recognize the divine spark within them. We consciously become part of the greater unity; we understand that they suffer as we do. We realize that their spark is dimmed due to suffering. Their violent actions are less about who they are and more based on their imperfections and the uncertain world.

As we move from affective empathy to cognitive empathy to compassionate action, community members, with their imperfections, become real to us. No longer strangers with incomprehensible beliefs and needs, they become integral, important parts of community. Our imperfections and theirs become opportunities to grow into a community of nonviolence.

A nonviolent community is an inclusive collective of many individuals with specific needs. No matter who joins us at the common table, we weigh their needs with the needs of others and the collective. Everyone is welcome and no one is denied a seat at the common table. This is the strength of a nonviolent community. All are welcome to become increasingly less violent as the collective grows into a nonviolent, compassionate community.

Decisions are made through intentional fact-finding and critical thinking. All members are encouraged to ask questions and be part of consensus building. In fact, members of a nonviolent community continuously ask questions in order to understand what is hindering the community from nonviolent living. Questions are not seen as threats to group stability but as opportunities to strengthen nonviolence at the core of community. It is understood that consensus building creates harmony.

The community celebrates what is working and views what is not working as opportunities, not obstacles, for growth.

Understanding is impossible without effective communication. Communication is paramount in a nonviolent community. In fact, the creation of a nonviolent community depends upon our ability to listen with intent and respond with compassion. As stated earlier, this is the core of communion — the cornerstone of nonviolent community. When we listen with intent, we focus on what is said, how it is said, and our reaction to it. So focused on the other and our reactions, we do not begin to formulate our response until the other is finished speaking.

Instead of judging what we feel is the most important aspect of what another said, we allow the entirety of the comments to settle into us. Once that person stops speaking, there is a moment of silence while we formulate our response. Then we compassionately share our thoughts. This type of communication, dialogue, requires moments of pause between two speakers. It requires intent to understand and to be understood.

Although initially this way of engagement may be uncomfortable, we do not rush to fill gaps of silence by reacting from fears or misunderstandings. It may not be until we have practiced dialoguing that we discover why we have disquieting feelings about what the other is saying. Instead of rushing to express our feelings, we listen to the four aspects of self — body, mind, spirit, and heart — to discover the reasons behind what we sense.

We listen to what another says and our somatic, mental, and emotional reactions to what is said. Next, we spend time quietly formulating our responses. Lastly, we respond from our compassionate center. We realize that we cannot fix our self, others, or the group. We empower our self, others, and the group through the practice of compassion directed to our self, themselves, and other group members.

Now it is your turn! Practice listening with intent and responding compassion.

**Practice:** Listen with Intent; Respond with Compassion

Engage in a conversation with someone. While they talk, clear your mind of any judgments, assumptions, or beliefs. Any questions that surface, let them go. Focus on what the person is saying verbally and nonverbally.

When your partner stops talking spend a few moments (15-45 seconds) collecting your thoughts to formulate your response.

Now respond.

- How did the conversation flow?
- How was this different of communicating from other conversations?

As a member of a nonviolent community, we are servant leaders. We lead by through our example and empowering others to leadership. Listening with intent and responding with compassion are traits of a servant leader. Humble and vulnerable, we do not hold our self above anyone. We are aware of individual imperfections and group imperfections yet do not judge. Imperfections and uncertainty are opportunities for growth. We encourage others and the group to be their best incarnation. With curious daring we share our best, truest self with the collective. With courage we listen to others. We share our truths while listening to the truths of others.

A servant leader guides by nonviolent example and empowers others to take leadership roles in community. They do not see themselves as a chief navigator on an uncertain voyage. Rather, they are one of Gandhi's many "drops in a limitless ocean of mercy" (Merton, loc 1311). One drop cannot quench the fire of violence, but many drops can tame the flames and illuminate the way to a more nonviolent existence.

As a servant leader we humbly expose our imperfections and encourage others to use their imperfections as teaching tools. We lead from with our authentic spirit. We know that collective nonviolence is only possible when we identify and tame the violence within our heart. We encourage others to identify and resolve the violence in their hearts. A servant leader knows what actions create and sustain a nonviolent community.

We acknowledge that each individual must begin to identify their roots of violent reaction before the collective can address any violence within itself. Individuals need not purge all the seeds of personal violence before creating a community of nonviolence — they must commit to the life long journey. To sustain a peaceful community, the discernment and purging of collective and individual violence must be ongoing.

Ongoing discernment is a trait of nonviolent resistance. We don't act in order to take a stand. Instead, each thought, word, and action is mindfully crafted to foster peace. Our attention is focused on being nonviolent despite our imperfections and the uncertainty in the world. This focused attention is the foundation of our resistance.

At the root of nonviolence is the sharing of our mystic heart. We no longer experience the world only cognitively. We experience the world from the messiness of emotions and triggers. We make sense of our experience with our head. Through focused attention, we become mystics with each experience. Or, as Dorothee Soelle believes, "resistance is not the outcome of mysticism, resistance is mysticism itself…" (Soelle, loc 2686). Resistance in a group requires the growth of a mystic collective heart.

A nonviolent community is a collaborative of mystics. We experience the sacred through the conscious connection of divine spark to divine spark. We choose nonviolence because any violence is anathema to our individual and collective authenticity. The more we live peacefully, the more we are aware how acts of violence impact us somatically, mentally, and emotionally. We are aware of the ways violence stresses our connection to all. Connection stressed, we are unable to be true bearers of peace and servant leaders in community.

A community of mystics is a community of mutual support. Together, we address the violence in the world. In times of stress, strength comes by empowering one another. Like one person modulating their breath and having others join in and creating a haven of peace, we can bring nonviolence by mindfully engaging a3 awareness — awake, alert, and alive in each moment — in our self and in community.

When hope and belief in a better, less violent way runs along our connections, collectively we are drawn to the many gates of nonviolence. We see the possibilities of a nonviolent, peace-filled world. We join together in consensus to create a world that gravitates toward nonviolence because that is the only viable option. We act in innovative ways to heal the woundedness in our self, others, the community, and the world.

As a community of mystics we intentionally experience life nonviolently within the gates of heaven. As a resident of community, our collective divine sparks connect to the originator of divine sparks, the Creator. Though this connection, we are inspired to act nonviolently. We discover the true location of the gate of nonviolence. It is in our body, mind, spirit, and heart.

Our understanding of violence shifts. While we never agree that violence is a viable option, we understand how violence grows from unchecked suffering. We are intentionally compassionate when others are imperfect and the world uncertain. Focusing our attention on the world, we acknowledge individual and collective fear at the root of violence. With this knowledge we courageously and peacefully confront violence.

Nonviolence is not a lofty goal or an hoped for result of community. Nonviolent communities exist. One such nonviolent community of mystics is the Quakers. They do not engage in confrontational resistance. Their resistance comes from a compassionate heart. Through history Quakers have acted in ways to unsettle the moral balance of perpetrators of violence. Quakers have been conscious objectors, stood in opposition to tyrants, and have lent their voice to the rights of immigrants. The foundation of this group is peaceful resistance that results in nonviolence in themselves, their community, and the world.

The Quakers are an example of internalizing the movement of nonviolence into a way of life. Movements come and go. Their purpose is to organize activities toward a goal. The Civil Rights Movement brought us to the cusp of equal rights in the United States. Often when a goal is realized, the movement is no longer a rallying force. We move on to another project. Eventually the power behind the movement is lost. We must begin anew. When we internalize a movement, we live it in our thoughts, words, and actions. When nonviolence becomes a way of life, we are mindful of when we, as a group or society, are reverting to violent ways.

We can choose to sustain a movement by integrating what we have learned into our way of life. This requires that we are ever vigilant in the ongoing achievement of the goal. We notice erosions of what we have gained. Instead of reacting violently to the loss, we work to reestablish the goals. This takes much diligence and energy. We must never believe that once we reach a goal that we need not act in ways that ensure its longevity.

When we choose to integrate the goals of the movement into our lived experience, we transform a movement into a way of life. These goals are the building blocks of transformation. A short term goal becomes part

of a long-term way of living. Integrating a movement into our way of life
ensure our transformation as individuals and as community. Through it,
we facilitate nonviolence in other aspects of our individual and collective
life.

Now it is your turn! Let's talk about movements and ways of life.

---

**Practice:** Movement vs. Way

A movement is an organization of activities toward a goal.
A way of life is sustaining what we have achieved into the whole of our
life and way of life.

- Do you agree or disagree with these definitions? Why?
- How have you integrated any movements into the way you live?

---

Being a mystic is a way of life. Being nonviolent is a way of life.
When we bridge our compassion aspirations to intentional, nonviolent
living, we live as a mystic resister. It is only when we join with other mystics that we gain the potential of nonviolent community. When an entire
community has a lived experience of nonviolence, we create a groundswell
of nonviolent possibility. Within that community lays the power of radical
transformation.

In living the way of nonviolence we recognize the truth in Gandhi's
words: "nonviolence heals and restores man's nature, while giving him a
means to restore social order and justice." (Merton, loc 556). The movement
heals and restores while the way provides the framework for social order and
justice. The mystic powers both the movement and the way through connection to others and the sacred. Neither movement or way is more important.
The movement provides the impetus to creating a lifelong way of living.

Through all of our efforts as a mystic, the sacred is woven. The
sacred is the ultimate movement — flowing, growing, driving within us. Our
mystical relationships with the sacred impels us to engage in nonviolent actions. Through these connections we weave the hope of nonviolence through
life's uncertainties. Through this way, we ignite the hope of nonviolence in
our individual and collective hearts. It becomes our first and only choice of
action — our way of life.

Merton cautions that in order to foster nonviolence in the world, "I do not laugh at my enemies, because I wish to make it impossible for anyone to be my enemy. Therefore I identify myself with my enemy's own secret self" (McDonnell, 502). We recognize how the imperfections of the so-called enemy are reflections of our imperfections. Think about that — how is an enemy's imperfection a reflection of your imperfections? How do these imperfections create the uncertainty in the world?

The world is a mirror for us. When we somatically understand this, we no longer seek to vilify but to compassionately understand. In understanding lays the potential to heal the wounds of our self, others, and community. With understanding, we welcome a collective of diversity into our community of nonviolence. We become a community of democratic mysticism.

We recognize that to be a democratic community we must respect the other where they are and expect respect from others. We cannot accomplish this unless we respect our self. Democracy begins with an investment from an individual who works in community. We grow our community's democratic nature by joining forces to realize the combined investments of individual members. We reap the benefits of a democratic community through consensus.

This form of community requires both collaboration and consensus. All are equal, all are leaders, all are perpetrators of both violence and nonviolence. We create this community when we "democratize mysticism by discerning it in the everyday forms of nonconformist life" (Soelle, loc 2816). Being nonviolent requires a degree of nonconformity — we willingly live our truth with curious daring and courageously share that truth with others. We accept the lived experience of others. In doing so, we become more comfortable with the uncertainty that comes from nonconformity.

No person is an island and to create silos of nonviolence ensures our defeat. When we create a community based upon a desire to be nonviolent while inviting diversity, we bridge these islands and tear down those silos. Only then can the woundedness caused by violence be healed. Together we live the way of a flourishing, nonviolent, democratic community. Our life truly is our message.

# Chapter 4

# My Life, My Message

We are imperfect. This is an indisputable fact. The world is uncertain — another indisputable fact. Yet, amid the imperfections and uncertainty, there is one constant — our divine spark. It connects us to the sacred in everything. All of our thoughts, words, and actions — violent and nonviolent — reverberate divine spark to divine spark. Think about that — every thought, word, and action impact your world. We choose to share our imperfections or to share our compassionate heart. We harm or we heal. Those are our only two choices.

With each thought, word, and action, we proclaim the words that Mahatma Gandhi said to a journalist who asked, "What is your message?" His reply was, "My life is my message." My life is my message might be the most powerful words that you ever own. In those words lay your truth. Spend time reflecting on what that means. What is your message?

Have you ever thought about the message your share? Perhaps it is the time, to take a moment at the end of each day, to reflect upon how you shared your message that day. You need not share your findings with anyone. This is about you evaluating your SCR and the ways you run up and down your Ladder of Inference. Through reflection you reframe your SCR to better represent your authentic self. A time of reflection empowers you to better align with the message of your authentic core.

We, consciously and unconsciously, choose this message we share. When we are unaware, it may or may not reflect our authentic intent. The reality is that as we navigate through uncertainty, our responses and reactions are our message even when they are warped by illusion and our reactions to those illusions. Although our intent is to share a message of peace and compassion, we get caught by our imperfections. We react. We become perpetrators of violence.

This detour into violence need not be forever. Instead of being caught in our reactions and spiraling into suffering, we mindfully acknowledge what hooks us. We disengage and forgive our self. We have to stop punishing our self for our imperfections. That gets us no where. Self compassion heals us. Through it we reframe our reactions into a compassionate responses. Our interactions become true reflections of our message.

When our life is our message, we practice a$^3$ awareness. We are awake to the world unfolding. We are alert to how our socially constructed reality (SCR) contributes to the casting of illusions and the feelings of uncertainty. We recognize that our SCR is not static. It is a flexible, dynamic, and evolving. If we are mindfully courageous and curiously daring, our SCR reflects our compassionate self. When we are unaware, it become crusted with illusion. As we become increasingly more aware, we let go of long-held beliefs and judgments based on illusions that prevent us from living authentically. We are alive.

As we evolve into our truest self, we are caught less in illusions. The fog of illusions clears, we see with new eyes — the eyes of a mystic. The gate of nonviolence becomes visible. With courage we enter the gate and build a life within it. In the gate we broadcast our message of peace and compassion through nonviolent action. Violence in any form unsettles us; it may also cause adverse reactions in our self. The more we live nonviolently, the greater we feel the angst that comes with violence.

As a mystic we transcend the world of structured uncertainty. We live in the gate of nonviolence, a place of our lived experience. We no longer live from only our heads. We experience life with our heart, move into our head to process what we experienced, and then respond through our heart. With hyperawareness we understand how the uncertainty in the world impacts us. While we may be imperfect, the strength of our mystic heart soothes any angst and fear we feel.

Our life becomes more than we ever expected. We sense the joys and the suffering in the world with equal intensity. We are compelled to stand as nonviolent, compassionate witness in an uncertain world. We are a compassionate healer soothing the world's woundedness. We know that we are imperfect. Although we intend to be nonviolent, we recognize that we are a work in progress. Any of our acts of violence are challenges to meet and lessons to learn. They are opportunities to practice compassion and reconciliation.

As a mystic, compassion and nonviolence is an experience of the heart. We integrate all four aspects of self (body, mind, spirit, and heart) as we move from our somatic and emotional experiences into cognition and then back to our lived experience. All beliefs are lived through experience. While we may articulate them in words and thoughts they do not grow cerebrally alone. Instead of explaining emotions, we dig deep into them to discover what triggered them.

With attention to the world and our response to it, our life truly becomes our message. Each of us, as mystic, sees each moment as opportunity to live our truth in each thought, word, and action. We reside in the gate of heaven knowing that unless we are mindful, we risk severing our connection to peace and solitude. No longer in peace, we slip into the commotion and uncertainty in the world. Within this uncertainty is the potential for personal violence. When we react out of fear, anxiety, or anger, we mirror our imperfections. The reflection of our mystic heart is clouded.

We are unable to enter the gate, much less take up residence, unless we are mindful. Even when we traverse the uncertainty into the extraordinary (the gate), we struggle to make the gate our permanent residence. Why? The ongoing commotion in the world is a constant onslaught. It erodes our mindfulness by feeding the fears at the roots of our imperfections. We get tangled in the commotion and fight our way out through reactions. But, with each reaction we get further tangled in the emotion. Our ability to respond weakens.

As the roots of fear and angst tangle, we lose awareness of the detrimental lasting effects of the commotion. We get fatigued. Our energy is diminished; our mind clouds. It becomes more difficult to be in the moment. We react in ways that do not represent our message. Any compassionate response remains just out of reach. Until we can acknowledge our fatigue, we continue to spiral into burnout. The way out of this cycle is to realign our body, mind, spirit, and heart using self compassion.

The way back to living a nonviolent life that truly represents our message is through self-compassion. If we do not care for our self, we lose the long-term ability to be compassion's presence in the world. Merton reminds us, "Action and contemplation become two aspects of the same things. Action is charity looking outward to other people, and contemplation is charity drawn inward to its own divine source. Action is the stream, and contemplation is the spring. The spring remains more important than the stream (Merton, 70). If our spring is depleted through a lack of self-compassion, our stream flows sluggishly. We do not have the resources to power our compassionate response. Our attempts to share compassion may not succeed. Our frustrated reactions may be violent.

Self compassion is not selfishness. Think of it as self care. We nurture our self so that we can share our truth with the world. When we are replenished it is easier to respond with clarity. We choose peace. Self compassion is an ongoing way of being. We cannot wait until we are depleted to nurture our self.

Not it is your turn! Let's create a self compassion routine.

---

**Practice:** Self Compassion

Self compassion need not take hours of time (although regularly taking a day for yourself is phenomenal!) Self compassion is self care. It may be:

- Taking a long bath
- Walking or hiking
- Journaling, coloring, or creating other forms of art
- Reading something you enjoy 30 minutes each day
- Practicing Tai Chi, yoga, or walking a labyrinth
- Pampering yourself with a pedicure or manicure
- Massaging lotion mindfully into your body
- Forgiving yourself
- Accepting that you are imperfect

Using any of the above or some specific practices of yours create a self compassion list to use throughout the week. You may designate specific days or may block time each day for self compassion time.

After a week ask yourself, "How did self compassion fill your spring and empower you to stream compassion to others?"

---

Self compassion is any activity that takes care of you. It is an act of self-love that alleviates your suffering and shields you from the world's uncertainties. Through self compassion we accept our imperfections as challenges to meet on the journey to authenticity. These acts recharge you. They fill the spring of your being so that you stream compassion. They are joy-filled moments of respite that refuel you. Through self compassion you are able to circumvent fear induced reactions and respond with compassion.

Although acts of self-compassion may be simple, they are not easy. Each act takes strength and courage. When we practice self-compassion, we are strong enough to put our self first no matter what others may say. We are humble in our admission that we need self-care and vulnerable in acknowledgement of our needs, small and large. As a result of caring for our self, we are more aware of our potential for violence. And, we recognize that, ultimately, the only person we can change is our self. In minimizing our potential for violence and maximizing our compassionate heart, we become a change agent whose actions are transformative.

Gandhi knew that passively watching from the sidelines and cheering on change would not address our imperfections and life's uncertainty. He encouraged each of us to be the change that we wish to see in the world. We are bringers of transformation when our actions reflect our intent. It may be scary to even think about being an active transformer, but the key to being a change agent is to integrate intent and action. Through knowing our self, we minimize the impact of our judgments and assumptions and become a clear channel for peace.

The integration of intent and action is the foundation of our life as our message. We choose how our actions reflect our authentic message. We no longer hold on to what does not serve us. We live in the moment, alert to opportunities to be a change agent. When our life is our message, we broadcast our authentic self in each action. We reside in the gate of nonviolence. Our shining light sparks transformation in our life and in the world.

Although we are aware of the propensity for violence in our self and others, we consciously respond with compassion when our life is our message. We navigate through the uncertainty with peace-filled calm. We do not meet violence with violence. To react violently becomes untenable. We feel the pain as it pierces through our body, mind, spirit, and heart. Our compassionate actions are a shield that protects us against the cruelty of the world.

Living our life as our message, we draw those who are on the mystic path to us. Eyes open, we become part of a field of a "billions of points of light" Merton talked about (Merton, 158). We feel the blaze of compassionate transformation fueled by a community of divine sparks. Within this collective we understand our mission is to cause no harm, to alleviate suffering, and to accept life in its current incarnation. This way of being, the three foundational awarenesses, is based upon Buddhist vows. By incorporating these three foundational awarenesses into our life, we become progressively less violent. They are discussed in detail in my book, *Engaging Compassion Through Intent and Action.*

*Cause No Harm:* Each of us has many imperfections. When we react from one, we inadvertently cause harm. Perhaps we are wounded so deeply that our first reaction is malicious. We cannot change past violent acts, but we can learn from them. We acknowledge the violence stemming from our actions, practice self-compassion while alleviating the suffering of those involved, and commit to causing no harm. We recognize that any reconciliation must include forgiving our self.

Agreeing to cause no harm, means living in a state of constant vigilance. We practice a$^3$ awareness: awake, alert, and alive to the potential of causing harm. Through awareness of our hurtful actions, we gain the ability to move past reactionary behavior into the default response of compassion. We consciously question our motives and see how they align with our intent. When they do not align, we address the harm we caused.

Now it is your turn! Let's see how your cause harm.

---

**Practice:** Cause No Harm

- For a day, notice your thoughts, your words, and actions. Keep notes. How do the seeds of your internal violence sprout within them?
- If you can, name what is at the root of the hurt/harm you perpetrate.
- Forgive yourself. Practicing self-compassion.
- Reframe your reactions to responses.
- Act compassionately toward the receiver of your violence.
- Notice how you felt mentally, emotionally, and somatically when you were nonviolent and compassionate.
- Name what informed both your reactions and responses.

---

*Be Compassionate*: The alleviation of suffering is the definition of compassion, the second foundational awareness. We recognize our biases that make it easier to practice compassion with certain people and ignore the suffering of others. We notice how we get attached to blaming or shaming another for their suffering. We recognize how we get stuck in our woundedness and judge someone undeserving of our compassion. When our life is our message, we are a practitioner of nonviolence. We recognize that we do not have to agree with the other person or even like the other to be compassionate.

Compassion is an act of unconditional love without expectations. This unconditional love, or the compassion of enough, alleviates suffering while holding the sufferer accountable for their actions. Compassion alleviates suffering — it does not ameliorate the consequences of our actions. We shift from compassion as a cure all to compassion as acceptance of our imperfections. Compassion does not restore us to our pre-suffering form; it returns us to wholeness. Each act of compassion prepares us to be streams of nonviolence.

We connect to one another, spark to spark, with each compassionate act. Through this network we rediscover the original unity — that we are all one. Our hearts beat in a community of mystic union. Through the healing power of compassion we create a community of nonviolence that radiates transformation into the world. We seed our message into the uncertain world. We do not change the world so much as we change the way we respond to it.

Now it is your turn!

**Practice:** Compassion As A Lived Experience

Compassion is simply an alleviation of suffering. Any acts that alleviate suffering are compassionate ones. (They may often masquerade as acts of kindness.) Do not let another negate your acts. Discover how compassion is your lived experience.

- What is your definition of compassion?
- List some ways you have been compassionate.

For a day,

- Notice the little and big ways you share compassion with others.
- Identify how others are compassionate to you.
- At the end of the day reflect on how you practiced self compassion.
- What surprised you?

How did these acts increase your response flexibility thus decreasing reactionary behavior?

---

*Life As It Is*: As an individual and as a community member, there are things we cannot change in the moment. Instead of regretting or fixating on past actions, our paradigm shifts. We accept our imperfections as challenges and lessons necessary to fully live with purpose. Within this paradigm, we are our most authentic self.

When we accept *life as it is*, the third foundational awareness, we are not complacent. Rather, we actively seek ways to live fully amid the uncertainty. Our boundaries become fluid and flexible. Life becomes an adventure that is lived through courage and curious daring. We live in ways that we might not have thought were possible. We understand that life is all about the journey not the destination. Each moment is an opportunity to learn from our imperfections and live our message.

While we are aware of our imperfections and the world's uncertainty, these no longer limit us. We reframe imperfections to challenges, that once met, deepen our nonviolent stance. These lessons teach us how to share compassion without judgment, attachment, or defense. We become an emissary of compassion in a deeply wounded world.

Instead of asking "why" we ask "why not" share compassion. Each time we act compassionately upon our "why not" answer, we are closer to living with authentic purpose. We more fully engage other points of light. We create a community of change agents committed to nonviolently transforming the world. Not only is our life our message, but, collectively, we become the change we reflect into the world.

Living authentically requires vulnerability, humility, courage, and trust. Gandhi named additional virtues "mercy, nonviolence, love, and truth in any person can be truly tested only when they are pitted against ruthlessness, violence, hate, and untruth" (Merton, loc 672). They are the roots of uncertainty in the world. Unless we live authentically, we get so tangled in the roots of violence that we cannot see past the uncertainty. The gate of nonviolence becomes invisible to our heart. We suffer. Our contact with our nonviolent essence blurs.

But, we need not remain disconnected from our authentic core. Our nonviolent heart can be resuscitated even if it has been strangled by imperfections and uncertainty in the world. We heal our heart, with loving, gentle thoughts, words, and actions — we practice self-compassion. Both Gandhi and Francis of Assisi recognized this way of healing. Gandhi said "Nonviolence cannot be preached. It has to be practiced" (Merton, loc 847). Francis of Assisi reminds us, "Preach the gospel. When necessary, use words." This practice is directed toward our self first.

Both invite us to get unstuck from the programming of being nice to the detriment of our self and others. We realize that being nice is not necessarily being compassionate. It can be an attempt at fixing or being codependent. Through compassion we bridge our intent and action. We empower others to bridge theirs. We create an interdependent community. Compassion is recognized as a tool to empower others to be their best, true self.

Nonviolence, like compassion, is never passive. Every thought, word, and action has the potential to be a nonviolent light that lessens fear and guides us through uncertainty. Through our compassion practice we unconditionally love while holding others accountable. Our life is a message of unconditional love, forgiveness, and justice. We encourage others to experience life in the same way. Compassionate action is the root of nonviolence.

Being loving, forgiving, and just requires mindfulness. Unless we are mindful, we may lose sight of "that of god" present in each person and each situation. Dorothee Soelle reminds us "that of god" may be "hidden, eclipsed, and forgotten" (Soelle, loc 2354). When our life is our message, we ignite the ember of remembrance within us. Then we consciously and intentionally seek that spark in others. We connect to "that of god" in every situation and in every person — even in times of violence. This transforms a community of judgment and victimization into a community of unconditional support.

---

**That of god** is the sacred reflected in those things that we hold in deep reference. It is the spark present in all. **That of god** is what we connect to when we practice compassion.

---

"That of god" is the sacred is present in all. For me, it may be in the gentle caring of someone or the kaleidoscopic colors of the sunrise. It is the root of every person's and every situation's ability to bring hope. When I connect to it, I am able to avoid reactionary violence and respond with love.

Now it is your turn! Where is "that of god" present in your life?

---

**Practice:** That of God

Even if you are not a religious or spiritual person, identify what you hold in deep reverence. Hold that knowing in your heart as you ask yourself:

- How is "that" present in me?
- How is "that" present in a loved one?
- How is "that" present in my community?
- How is "that" present in the "other"?

How does your identification of the commonality of "that" in yourself and others encourage you to shift your thoughts, words, and actions from violence to nonviolence?

---

As a mystic whose lived experience is nonviolence, we realize the we are never alone. For we "walk joyfully on the earth and respond to that of god in every human being" (Soelle, loc 2356). Relationship connects our compassionate heart and nonviolent spirit to others and sustains us in the uncertainty. We do not objectify or "other" another person. We befriend them by welcoming them into a community where there is room for all. In doing so, we create a nonviolent, inclusive community that celebrates diversity.

Experiencing the way of nonviolence as a mystic means we are never alone. This knowing connects our compassionate heart and nonviolent spirit to others. Our life and our message shines a swatch through uncertainty. Living authentically through our message, we friend others by welcoming them into a community where there is room for all. We create a nonviolent, inclusive community that celebrates diversity. In doing so, we become "that of god."

In this inclusive community we are all servant leaders who lead through gentle dialogue and by example. In doing so, we develop a new relationship to our lived experience. We encourage, by our example, others to deepen their lived experience of nonviolence. We are mystics fully present in the gate of nonviolence. The gate is not a hermitage. We invite individuals and communities to join us in the place of nonviolence. No one is barred from admittance. All are invited to experience the mystic life.

Rooted in the present moment, we recognize that we experience life holistically — physically, emotionally, mentally, and spiritually. We engage our body, mind, spirit, and heart by living in a3 awareness. Hyperaware we are poised to avoid reactionary triggers. We respond with compassion. When we give our self unreservedly to the present moment, we recognize that this is the only moment we have. We can be compassionate and nonviolent or we react out of our imperfections and the world's uncertainty.

Mindfully we are attentive to the world around us. We recognize the unity of contemplation and action is nonviolence. In a state of nonviolence, we move from spectator to participant. We speak and act in ways that alleviate suffering. Our thoughts, words, and actions reduce the impact of violence on our self, others, and the world.

As we practice slow, even breathing, we gain the power to empower others to shift from reaction to reflective quiet. We exude calm. We are peace in our demeanor. Our voice has a peace pitch and our physical movements are graced. Nonviolence permeates our body, mind, spirit, and heart. Even if we do not speak, we share the message that transformation is possible.

When our life is our message, we intuitively bridge our intent with our action. The forming of this bridge is possible only in the present moment. We consciously create and maintain this bridge though practice. The following five steps create an arc from intent to action. These five steps are *intentio, meditatio, oratio, contemplatio*, and *actio*. (The middle three stages of the process are part of an ancient way of praying, *Lectio Divina*.)

- *Intentio* is the conscious intent of how we wish our authentic self be reflected in our actions. We affirm our intent at the beginning of our day. It may be reset throughout the day as a reminder of our life message. Intent is the internal articulation of our external message.

- *Meditatio* is focusing our awareness on the sacred or what we hold in reverence. In this state we are open to acting upon information that helps us to live more compassionately. The practice of *meditatio* results in information that helps us move from being reactionary to compassionately responsive.

- *Oratio* is our prayer or petition. It comes from our strong desire to gain clarity and accept that we are imperfect in an uncertain world. Through *oratio*, we acknowledge imperfections in our self and others while sharing compassion. Amid the world's uncertainty, we dialogue with the sacred through our divine spark. We speak; the Creator listens.

- *Contemplatio* is the second part of this dialogue with the sacred. It is quiet listening. In *oratio* we speak with the tongue of our soul. During *contemplatio* we intentionally listen with our heart. Our desire is to discern the next steps on the journey of transformation in an uncertain world. Through *contemplatio* we use full body listening as we engage the world with all of our senses.

- *Actio* is our response. It reflects the many ways we engage the world with our thoughts, words, and actions. When they align with our intent, our divine spark shines its light into the world with the brilliance of compassion and peace.

When we live from *intentio* to *actio*, we echo the words of Meister Eckhart, "what we have gathered in contemplation, we give out in love" (Soelle, loc 2716). Both nonviolence and compassion are acts of love that soothe the uncertainty and bring compassion to the imperfections.

When I first practiced *intentio* to *actio*, it took a conscious effort to stay in the moment aware and open. Then something curious happened. I found myself living from *intentio* to *actio*. It was engrained in my being. So, it can be with you. With practice and awareness your life can be your message through the arc of your intent and action.

Not it is your turn! Let's practice *intentio* to *actio*.

---

### The Practice of *Intentio* to *Actio*

Spending some time in quiet. Allow your breath to flow where you are tense. Relax. When you are ready, ask

"What is my *intentio*?"
- Close your eyes, ask, "what is my message?"
- Notice your breathing as the answer surfaces

Enter into *meditatio*
- Turn your awareness to the moment
- How are you being invited to manifest your intent?
- What distractions are barriers to your intent?

Move to *oratio*
- Reformulate your intent
- Fashion your *oratio* with both your intent and your awareness of your distractions

Enter into *contemplatio*
- Listen to your inner wisdom
- Be without words…listen with all your body
- Understand what you are given

Practice your *actio*

Throughout the day, ask yourself:
- What is stopping me from creating an arc from my intent and action?
- How am I integrating all five steps into my daily lived experience?

---

With each arc of *intentio* to *actio* we cultivate our mystic heart. We listen with the ear of our heart and respond with the voice of our soul. Eventually we sustain a bridge of intent and action. Walking this bridge as a mystic warrior, we no longer hold on to petty grievances. Our need for revenge lessens. Fully engaged in a³ awareness, we understand what matters — being peace and love in an uncertain world. We are warriors who hold the peace and diminish the need for war.

We understand that nonviolence is a choice — we can be a warrior of peace or a warrior of destruction. In *oratio*, we choose peace. We act nonviolently, and in doing so, transform our self and the world. *Contemplatio* is the great listening that provides guidance as we move through the angst of imperfection and into compassionate action. From *intentio* to *actio*, our life is truly our message.

This five-step process is best integrated into the whole of your life. During this mystic practice, identify episodes of arrogance and attachment to things, people, and ideas. Recognize how your imperfections and the world's uncertainty feed your violence. Let go of attachments, release those things that keep you stuck in violence. Although *intentio* to *actio* guides you into along the path of nonviolence, you may use the process to discover how you get caught in our imperfections and react violently.

When our life is our message, we become a servant who leads by example. We are a peace navigator through an uncertain world. We lead with our courageous heart and attain the goal of compassionate presence: "to become free from oneself and all things" (Soelle, loc 2887). Through humility and the release of attachments, we rest more certainly in the gate of nonviolence. In this freedom we are courageously nonviolent and compassionate.

When our life is our message we are free from the illusion that tells us we are forever bound to our imperfections. We finally realize that at any moment we can choose the way we want to live. Free to connect, divine spark to divine spark, we create a web of possibility. This web is strung with the twinkling lights of nonviolence and compassion.

When our life is our message we free our self from the illusion that forever binds us to our imperfections. We realize that at any moment we can choose the way we want to live. We are free to connect, divine spark to divine spark. We live within a web of possibility. This web is alive with nonviolence and compassion.

We are reminded that we are "the vessel. The draught is god. And god is the thirsty one" (Soelle, 3092). Our life is our message becomes the water that relieves the *thirst of that of god*. In meeting our challenges and learning our life lessons we create a stronger, more durable connection to the sacred manifest in the divine spark within all. We recognize that the sacred not only connects us to the creator; it is the water that quenches our thirst to live nonviolently.

For the mystic, "our spiritual life is first of all our life" (Merton, 37). All that we do reflects our relationship with the sacred. With a commitment to nonviolence, we are ever vigilant that our thoughts, words, and actions are reflections of our humble heart. We live with one foot in the extraordinary, the gate of nonviolence, while the other is in the uncertain world. We share nonviolence and compassion birthed in the gate with the world.

Each nonviolent act is an invitation to reside in the gate of nonviolence while inviting others to join us. We may not be able to change life's uncertainty, but we learn to rise and fall with its ebb and flow. We may never be perfect, but we accept our imperfections as tools of transformation. We accept that while our life may never be perfect, our response is always a reflection of our message.

Living in the gate, the place of the nonviolent connection, requires a bridge from divine spark to divine spark. The Sufis saw this as a journey. Thomas Merton saw it as a loving relationship. The following is a reflection of these ways of seeing life based upon information about Sufis taken from *Silent Cry Mysticism and Resistance* and Thomas Merton's quote from *Thoughts in Solitude*. Both invite us to walk the mystic path of nonviolent resistance.

Sufism: *Journey to God: is awakening from ordinary sleep with the awareness of exile. This awakening finds us in the valley of seeking* (Soelle, Loc 1089).

Thomas Merton: *Those who live for God, live with other people and live in the activities of their community. Their life is what they do* (Merton, 117).

This initial way of being is an awakening to the knowing that we are imperfect in an uncertain world. Our heart feels the suffering of our self, others, and the world. Instead of remaining lost in uncertainty, we acknowledge god at the center of our being. We seek to live in ways that reflect that connection of divine spark to divine spark.

Sufism: Journey in God: *the human ego has been extinguished through self-annihilation. We rest in the valley of love.*
Thomas Merton: *Those who live with God also live for God, but they do not live in what they do for God, they live in what they are before God. Their life is to reflect God by their own simplicity and by the perfection of God's being reflected in their poverty.*

Entering into *meditatio* and *oratio*, we recognize that at our core is that is of god — our divine spark. All that we do is a reflection of this essence. We actively seek ways to be with others in community as we live with God in ways that are reflected in the divine sparks of all creation. Our message is reflected in the flickering of our divine spark reflected in others and the world.

Sufism: *Journey through God: the search that God has begun and caused without which the human search is unthinkable. We seek truth in the valley of knowledge.*
Thomas Merton: *Those who live in God do not live with others or in themselves still less in what they do, for God does all things in them.*

This is the path of the mystic. We transcend boundaries through the recognition that we are not separate entities; we are part of the original unity. We consciously celebrate this unity. Our personal relationship with the sacred evolves and expands. We live in relationship knowing that there is a third partner in all relationships. That partner? The sacred. And, we recognize that our nonviolent and compassionate actions are not ours alone. They are a reflection of that of god, our divine spark. Living in this way, our life becomes our message.

The journey through God or living in God blurs the line between the world of uncertainty and the gate of nonviolence. We live in the uncertain world while acting with nonviolent and compassionate convictions found in the gate. Our thoughts, words, and actions reflect the joy and compassion found within the gate. We use the power of anger to move us from the uncertainty to unconditional love and compassion. The force of anger no longer controls our actions. As Dorothee Soelle reminds us, "the more we let go of our false desires and needs, the more we make room for amazement in the every day life" (Soelle, loc 1312). We have no desire to be violent for we know the joys and happiness that come from living in the gate of nonviolence.

Now it is your turn! How do you live?

---

**Practice:** How do you live?

Reflect upon the words of the Sufis and Thomas Merton. Choose the way that best fits how you are currently living.

- Which best describes how you live?
- How does this way contribute to growing your nonviolent heart?
- How does this way perpetuate violence in your thoughts, words, and actions?

- Which way resonates more with you?
- How does it encourage or prevent nonviolence?
- Could you see yourself shifting into another way of being?
- If so, why?
- If so, how?

---

Nonviolence and compassion are the paving stones on the mystic path. When our life is our message, nonviolence is ultimately our response to a world that is imperfect and uncertain. We recognize that within us is the power to radically change the world through our transformation. The sacred is the movement that resonates to our authentic core. It sparks a longing to adopt the way of nonviolence and compassion. The sacred flames our divine spark. In the flare of the sacred, we burn away any desire to react to life's uncertainty and imperfections. We reside in the gate of nonviolence fully connected to the original unity. We live the way of nonviolence and compassion. Only then is our life truly our message.

# Afterword

The uncertainty in the world causes so much commotion. Our personal imperfections get triggered by this commotion. Without an awareness of who we are, we are stuck in the mire of our internal violence exploding outward. But, this need not be. We can adopt a new way of being. We accept that we are imperfect and use our imperfections as lessons. Meeting challenges and learning lessons unlock the gate of nonviolence. Gate thrown open, we join with others to create a community of nonviolence and compassion. We return to the older unity. With a commitment to our authentic self, our life becomes our message — a message of hope, compassion, peace, and reconciliation.

I hope you found this workbook helpful as your journey the pathway to your nonviolent, compassionate lived experience. Perhaps, within the covers, you found gems of wisdom that furthered you along the path of peace and compassion. Maybe you recognized others ways to live your message that are not found within these pages. This is about your journey and discovering your way. It is not about creating a replica of my journey.

We are well past the crossroads where our choice of direction would have little impact on our lives and the lives of others. We have a choice. Our actions can drive us deeper into the desolate land of schisms caused by violence or we can choose to work the compost of reconciled past actions into the arid land. Fertile once again, we can sow seeds of peace and compassion. Within that fertile land, schisms heal.

Your message, your choice. The time to make a choice is every moment of every day of the rest of our life. May you, and I, choose to act nonviolently as individuals and collectively so that our life truly is our message of hope, peace, and compassion. May your message, and mine, transform the world.

Looking forward in peace and compassion,
Vanessa

# Resources

Burton. N. Asian Journal of Thomas Merton, ed. Naomi Burton, Brother Patrick Hart, and James Laughlin ,(New York: New Directions, 1973)

Chödrön, P. Practicing Peace in Times of War Shambala. 2014.

– – –. Start Where You Are: A Guide to Compassionate Living (Shambhala) 2001

McDonnell. P. ed. A Merton Reader (New York: Image Books, 1989)

Merton. T. Conjectures of a Guilty Bystander. New York: Image.

– – –. ed. Gandhi On Nonviolence. New York: A New Directions Book. ebook

– – –. Faith and Violence, Notre Dame: University of Notre Dame Press: 1968

– – –. No Man Is An Island (New York: Harvest Book, 1983

– – –. Seeds of Contemplation. (Norfolk, CT: New Directions Books, 1949)

– – –. The Springs of Contemplation: A Retreat at the Abbey of Gethsemani (Notre Dame, Indiana: Ave Maria Press, 1992)

Merton. T. Thoughts in Solitude. (New York: Farrar, Strauss, Giroux)

Rosenberg, M.B. (2015) Nonviolent Communication: A Language of Life Puddle Encinitas, CA: Dancer Press ebook

Soelle, D. 1997. The Silent Cry: Mysticism and Resistance. Minneapolis: Fortress Press. ebook

Williamson, M. 1992 A Return to Love: Reflections on the Principles of "A Course in Miracles"